AGENT MASTERMIND

BY

SCOTT HUDSPETH & TEAM

AGENT MASTERMIND

Ordering Information:
Quantity sales. Special discounts are available on quantity purchases by corporations, associations, and others.
Orders by U.S. trade bookstores and wholesalers. Please contact SCOTT HUDSPETH via
https://www.agentmastermind.com

Edited and Marketed By
DreamStarters University
www.DreamStartersUniversity.com

Table of Contents

DEDICATION

I dedicate this book to my amazing wife Stacey Hudspeth and my two incredible kids, Lexie Hudspeth and Greg Hudspeth. They have been my biggest fans and my number one WHY!

The reason I do everything I do is for my family.
Thank you, guys!

Much love, Dad

Doug Cadaret established the Cadaret Mortgage Group in 1996. He built a 20+ million dollar a year origination practice that was 100% referred based on the Triangle of Trust Mindset. As a result, 63% of our annual business comes from past and current clients.

"We are the most preferred lender because we are the most referred lender." The Cadaret Mortgage Group currently has offices in MI and FL.

"While I spend most of my time coaching LO's and Real Estate Agents and speaking for groups, Denise, my wife runs the day-to-day operation of the mortgage practice."

Chapter 1

How To Get More Referrals

I'm Doug Cadaret, and since 1996, I have been a referral-based mortgage consultant. From day one, I have grown and managed my practice, the Cadaret Mortgage Group, using only one business model: Believing that the definition of a successful transaction is the right to earn a referral before closing.

Here I will share my secrets so that you can develop strategies to successfully build trusting relationships that result in referrals. Just picture it -- you'll never have to advertise again, it will all be done through word-of-mouth.

First, Find Success in Your Personal Life

Before you're able to put your best foot forward and show up to your client in the most referable way, you need to find balance in your personal life. To do this, I suggest that you practice integral living.

Take a personal evaluation of various areas of your life to include physical, spiritual, social, family, psychological, and recreational, to name a few. Much like a wheel needs air to roll smoothly, you need balance across the board to be successful. The more balance you have in your personal life the more attractive and present you become to your work life.

You need to have a great life and insert a successful business into it -- it doesn't work the other way around. How you spend your time is crucial. As Annie Dillard said, "How we spend our days is, of course, how we spend our lives." Strive for balance.

Be Successful in Your Professional Life

I want to talk about survival versus significance.

When you're new to real estate or lending, you're in a self-centric survival mode and your work is a means to pay the bills. In other words, it's just a job.

As you begin to put systems in place, you take your focus off surviving, and your start to believe that this is a viable career. This stability frees you from the ups and downs of simply surviving and allows a movement towards creating intentional conversations and actions that amplify your relationships.

Once these systems start to create raving fans from your referral partners, current clients and past clients, your focus can move to expanding your brand and your real estate or lending practice becomes a successful business.

Finally, when you're at a point where you can devote more time to sharing your knowledge and mentoring others, you've achieved significance. Your priorities expand and you experience new satisfaction.

This requires big thinking. I want you to move away from the tasks that were once your job to move toward making this your career, your calling. Stop engaging in the basic tasks and start focusing on money-making activities.

Think of it this way -- would you rather wake up everyday and go to a J-O-B or walk into a business and be a leader for others?

My Secrets to Success

Once you decide how to spend your time, you'll want to manage it well. It is for this reason I suggest the following actions:

1. **Be intentional.** You deserve your clients' endorsement to the people they care about. Being intentional is the catalyst for referable behavior. In the course of your everyday business life, you'll have many opportunities to ask for referrals. Learn to recognize these opportunities and be aware of what language and behaviors encourage referrals.

2. **Set boundaries.** There is no need to be available 24/7. Set the stage early in the process about your hours. You'll be pleasantly surprised at how many people will respect those boundaries and work with you. Keep in mind that you can always make exceptions to these hours.

3. **Assess and create a referable environment.** In order to improve your referability, you need to create an environment for growth. Ask yourself the following questions: What five things in my environment am I most proud of / lower my self-esteem / require change / or will help me reach my goals? Regularly assess and make changes as necessary to stay on track.

4. **Develop and practice scripts**. Remember, there's only one thing that separates you from your competition, the words that you speak. Are your presentations and language designed to setting the stage to create moments of referability?

5. **Answer the question of "WHY?"** There's a white elephant in every conversation that needs to be addressed by you. Why should you be the one your clients choose to work with? If you can't clearly answer this question for your clients, they won't be able to either.

6. **Create a brand.** The Triangle of Trust is a brand. It is an act of helping others, and amplifying relationships without demanding anything in return so that we invoke the power of reciprocity. Clients who are treated well will want to do good for you in return -- including referring you as a trusted professional.

10 Guidelines to Develop Your Referability

If you had a choice, would you rather work with a referral or a lead? If you are like most of us, working with a referral is preferred. Think of the last client that was referred to you and how that process looked and felt.

Choose to seek out "Moments of Gratitude" in your work. Meaning, look for those moments where the people you talk to say, "Thank you," "That was awesome," "I appreciate that," "Wow." Basically, anytime someone shows you appreciation, ask them for help in introducing you to someone they care about.

Commit to seeking this in all of your conversations and treating others, not as you would like to be treated, but rather how they would want to be treated. This is the most effective choice to build your business to new levels and keep it there for a long time to come.

I'd like to conclude by providing you with guidelines to implement in your business in order to get the referrals necessary to build and maintain a great future.

1. Know the Anatomy of a referral: Make a connection + Set the stage + Create Gratitude by adding value + Ask for an introduction = A referral.
2. Respect your and your clients' time.
3. Set the stage about your brand before anything else. Don't just be "Google" for your clients.
4. Establish boundaries that create a referable environment.
5. Be more interested than interesting.
6. Acknowledge people frequently with handwritten, personal notes.
7. Learn to capitalize on the moments of gratitude you receive from your clients during the process.
8. Actively invite feedback. Give people permission to share how they feel about your service.
9. Don't be afraid to ask for the business. You can say, "Don't keep me a secret!"
10. Speak with confidence and passion, deliberately selecting your words.

The key to improving your referability is to become more proactive and less reactive. Utilize these steps and your referrals and business will elevate to a more enjoyable and profitable level.

"Define a successful transaction as earning a referral before closing, choose to create and work with referrals and not leads, and clearly know why you are referable."

Doug Cadaret

As a real estate agent for over 20 years, **Michael Hellickson** consistently listed and sold over 100+ homes per month and now coaches agents and brokers of all production levels with Club Wealth® Coaching and

Consulting™. He and his wife Tara live in Seattle, Washington with their children, Madison and Austin, and two English Pointers.

Chapter 2

Lead Conversion and Listing Presentation

I'm Michael Hellickson, and I want to set you apart from the competition. For more than 20 years, I've been a successful real estate agent who has consistently listed and sold over 100+ homes per month. I now coach agents and brokers of all production levels with Club Wealth® Coaching and Consulting™.

I'll share the reasons why 87% of agents fail in the first five years, how to avoid those pitfalls, and how to find personal and professional success. I'll share the hottest lead sources and my strategy to follow up, which converts virtually every time.

To start, I want you to know our core value at Club Wealth: "No success in the world can compensate for failure in the home." When you're setting out, establish what it will require for you to earn a living. If necessary, build a strong and reliable team around you. If you don't have anyone helping with your professional pursuits, then it's all you, all the time. Unfortunately, something will have to give, and that something that often suffers is your family. I want you to come in knowing exactly how to tackle this industry, and do it in a way that will allow you to achieve balance in both your personal and professional lives.

When it comes to success, I want to impart that success DEMANDS work! Beware of magic pills, stop listening to negative people, and don't get stuck. It's easy to fall into the traps of either becoming a professional learner or spending way too much time "getting ready to get ready." Although lifelong education and skill acquisition are valuable, do not let them stop you from *doing* -- action is key.

Top Reasons Agents Fail

None of us set out to fail, so it's important to avoid these pitfalls:

- Bad habits/lack of good habits
- Showing up to work "whenever"
- Finding excuses not to work
- Confusing "busy work" for "dollar productive work"
- Acting as firemen/women; always reactive, not proactive

I would like to impart this wisdom to you: you need to take control of your schedule, because our habits dictate our results.

At Club Wealth®, we offer a variety of no-cost online checklists with step-by-step activities to follow, so that you can properly utilize your time and successfully plan your days and goals. If you're asking yourself, "What activities do I need to do to make $150k to $200k per year?" then visit ClubWealth.com/pds. All you need to do is follow the checklist, and success and money will follow.

The Importance of Leads

Let's make it simple -- 90% of your day needs to be dedicated to the following three things:

1. **Lead generation.** Here is the exciting news -- you don't have to chase business, you can attract business. When it comes to lead generation, 61% of the average agent's business comes from their sphere of influence. I recommend you host four client events per year (such as a backyard BBQ), and utilize calls, social media posts, online groups, and pop-bys if you have time and are just starting out.

2. **Lead follow up.** The fortune is in the follow up. Do you know how long you have to follow-up with an online lead? Exactly 20 seconds. If not, it's gone and someone else will take it. We actually tested this in California. In the first five minutes, leads will receive calls from five agents. One particular agent would call the lead and stay on the line for five minutes so that the other agents would immediately go to voicemail -- it was pretty clever. I recommend this formula: Call your leads three times a day for the first three days, three times a week for the next three weeks, and three times a month for the next three months.

3. **Lead conversion.** Focus your efforts into closing and transitioning these leads into satisfied clients. Don't get stuck working on your brand, designing flyers, etc. Instead, focus on your leads and you will earn a much higher income. I highly recommend that you outsource administrative tasks so that you can play to your

strengths and focus on the money-making activities.

Obtaining New Leads

As you've learned, the best lead source is your sphere of influence. You need to learn to get business in other ways too, so that you increase the number of transactions while decreasing the work.

The #1 paid seller lead source on the planet is LeadsLikeCandy.com. We use this every single day and it covers every single market.

There are well over 2,000 lead sources in real estate today. Clearly, some deliver better ROI than others. We've narrowed that list down to about 112. Due to space limitations, and the rapidly changing nature of what works TODAY, visit www.ClubWealth.com/blog where we consistently update you with our favorite lead sources. In the meantime, make sure you add at least one new lead source to your business every 3 months.

My Personal Secret to Success

If I had to sum it up in one word, it would be *tenacity*. I have aggressively gone after my goals. When I said that the fortune is in the follow up, I want you to know that there have been times in my career where I made 115-120 follow-up calls per day. Others weren't doing that. This is what it took to succeed at that level.

Additionally, play to your strengths. For example, if you are the lone ranger agent competing against a big team, say this to your potential client: "With me you always know who you're working with. I'm going to take care of you and serve you like no other." Service is the number one thing that you can provide better than everyone else. You might not have the experience or the numbers yet, but you can over-serve your clients, and I highly recommend it.

I recommend high levels of service, because everyone wants individualized attention. You have to be selfless, not self-serving. Become a servant instead of a sales person.

Remember to work your sphere of influence, acquire new leads, and follow the checklists for success available online at ClubWealth.com. And when it comes to your follow ups, call them three times a day for the first three days, three times a week for the next three weeks, and three times a month for the next three months.

If you do things that your competition can't or won't, you'll set yourself apart and enjoy immense success. What you can conceive and believe, you can achieve!

"Everyone loves the exclusivity of off-market homes."

Michael Hellickson

Michael LaFido, the founder of the Marketing Luxury Group, assists other real estate agents and affluent homeowners by providing top-tier services including consulting, lifestyle marketing, public relations and coaching to help agents and owners sell their luxury homes; utilizing our proven and reputable strategies.

While many Realtors struggle to break into the luxury niche, it was relatively easy for LaFido once he introduced potential clients to fresh strategies like event- based marketing and videos featuring professional actors. This natural marketer readily admits to looking outside the real estate industry for ideas, transforming proven concepts into methods that have modernized luxury realty.

Michael has created the nationally recognized luxury certification for real estate agents which is known as Luxury Listing Specialist (LUXE). This new certification establishes an in-depth and detailed set of standards for agents that represent luxury homes, and is currently offered for 12 hours of Continuing Education (CE) for real estate agents in Texas. The trainings are based on the same principles Michael outlines in his book, *Marketing Luxury* that he teaches to agents across the world. Many agents and brokers are calling Michael's systems "The New Standard" for marketing luxury homes today.

Chapter 3

How to Break Into & Dominate Selling High-End Homes

Have you ever dreamed about breaking into the luxury market?

I'm Michael LaFido, an industry-renowned luxury listing specialist and bestselling author. I will share with you my top three steps to make more money in the next year without adding any additional work to your plate. My proven techniques will allow you to break into the higher-end market and dominate it.

This training chapter is perfect if you want more luxury listings and buyer clients, are open to new marketing strategies and want to differentiate yourself from your competition. I will share with you proven and repeatable systems and a fresh new approach to selling luxury real estate.

Why Break In To the Luxury Market

I want to tell you a little about myself. I am a husband, a father of three and a former PE teacher. When I first broke into real estate, my commission in the first five years equated

SCOTT HUDSPETH & TEAM

to $43,542. That breaks down to an average of $8,708/year. I needed more income.

I then realized the value of going after higher-value properties. I had three options to double my income: sell more homes; increase what I charged; and/or increase my average sale price. I believe increasing the average sale price of a home is the fastest way to double your income.

If you put your current selling efforts into higher-end homes, you'll:

1. Earn higher paychecks
2. Become more profitable
3. Experience better ROI
4. Receive better referrals
5. Enjoy more time off
6. Establish credibility/respect
7. Love what you do

Have I sold you on the concept yet? If you're wondering where to get started, I want to begin with three simple steps to success: establishing your foundation; designing your blueprint; and marketing through video.

New Thinking, New Strategies

Here is a new concept for you -- Don't think like a real estate agent, think like a marketer. Change your way of thinking to yield new results in your business. The good news for you is that there are lots of traditional agents, or as I like to call them "dinosaur agents," who are operating on the same systems they always have, without embracing new strategies.

I want you to also push aside your fears and misconceptions of this market. Many agents believe that this market is difficult to break into because luxury sellers will rarely give you their business until you can show them you have sold similar listings in their area. This is not true.

Other misconceptions include that you personally need to be wealthy, drive a nice car, live in a big home and need to be affiliated with a specific office. I'm going to tell you how to push these aside and how to break into this illustrious and exciting market.

Build Your Foundation

You are your greatest asset and I truly believe that in order to succeed, you need to strengthen your "inner game." Know that through your past, you have developed muscles not wounds. Perhaps it's my former career as a PE teacher, but I want to say, "You can do it!" Provide yourself with similar positive self-talk and affirmations. Once you do this, you'll be ready to step out of your comfort zone.

In order to strengthen your confidence, you need to increase your personal knowledge. Learn what gives you the advantage and be able to articulate it, develop people skills, and become more likeable.

Next go beyond yourself. Develop a knowledge of your client, your competition and your numbers. Create data and graphs that articulate data for luxury real estate in your area and get to know the price point at which luxury listings begin. From there, align yourself with luxury affiliates and become a student of local luxury trends.

Combine these and you will feel more confident, which will improve your sales abilities.

Design Your Blueprint

It is now time to position yourself as the Luxury Specialist. You'll do this through marketing. I want you to know that the first rule of marketing is attention -- attract your clients, don't chase them.

All clients care about one thing: "What's in it for me?" Remember this when designing your message and the ways in which you conduct yourself in interactions. As the great Theodore Roosevelt said, "Nobody cares how much you know until they know how much you care."

Although this market has a tremendous amount of earning potential, it is a much smaller market. So how do you break in? In order to get their attention and influence the influencers, you need to create unique experiences or services. I advise that you create a Luxury Networking Group.

I recommend that you serve as the connector, invite non-competing luxury clients and meet once per month. Ideas of members include individuals in the following arenas:

- Interior Designers
- Luxury Stagers
- Luxury Cars
- Luxury Clothing/Stores
- Luxury Home Improvement
- Home Theatre
- Artwork/Jewelry/Restaurant
- CPA/Divorce Atty/Tax Appeal

Meetings can include member introductions, interviews, what's working, establishing who the ideal client is, and identifying areas you need help with. Take this base and invite members to your events and open houses, via evites, email, text and video.

Market with Video

The most effective tool you can utilize to promote yourself, your services, your properties and your brand is video. In fact, 73% of sellers say they would hire an agent who uses video to market their home over an agent who doesn't use video.

Video will differentiate you from competitors. You're able to easily show and tell a property or event, build trust, and quickly share across your social media channels, which will encourage shares. Your clients can access video from mobile devices while on the go, and Google loves video for visibility. Videos are desirable from both buyers and sellers and are very easy to consume. Trust me, you'll love the return on investment this medium will provide you.

Utilize Facebook Live and create a YouTube Account. Your videos can be brief, and can be shot in one take. Some topics you may want to include are:

- Tips for buyers and sellers
- Tips for investors
- Tips for homeowners and renters
- Market updates
- Tips for future sellers or buyers

The luxury real estate market is highly lucrative with new opportunities and possibilities. Utilize my simple steps to break into the industry, boost your confidence, get connected and become the luxury specialist in your market.

"The most effective tool you can utilize to promote yourself, your services, your properties and your brand is video."

Michael LaFido

Jason Morris has been an active real estate agent in the Myrtle Beach, SC market since 2004.

"I had no sphere of influence and I was a broke right-out -of-college kid that drove an old pick up truck. A few months into the real estate business I discovered telephone prospecting. I quickly became one of the top agents in my office.

During the last 14 years, I have been a successful agent, no matter what the market conditions were. In 2016, I started the Facebook group "Real Estate Agents That REALLY Work" because I saw there was a need in the industry for someone to teach real estate agents how they can build a highly profitable business without a lot of overhead or working seven days a week."

For more information, visit www.JasonMorrisGroup.com

Chapter 4

How to Get Listings In A Tough Market

Every market has its ups and downs, and real estate is certainly no exception. I'm Jason Morris, a real estate agent out of South Carolina, and I specialize in generating consistent listings, especially in a tough market.

In difficult times, it is more important than ever to find your niche, to discover new marketing methods, and to explore how you can separate yourself from the competition.

I'm going to share with you how to get more listing leads, along with a comprehensive follow- up system that you can implement immediately.

When you're in a tough market, you'll either be crushing it and getting listings left and right, or struggling to find your niche because there are more experienced agents in the market, and you end up getting shut out.

I've got some bad news -- in the coming years, expect to start competing against things you may not have considered. You'll encounter changes in technology, downward pressure on commissions, more agents with less experience, third-party companies coming into your market, home flipping shows, and far more distractions than ever before. This will especially factor if you utilize social media networks to market your business.

27

How to Succeed

Now let's get to the good news -- here are the tools you'll need to get listings in this tough market:

Focus on your daily schedule

You must have a schedule and follow it. As we get busier, it's easy to get pulled away from money-making activities. You'll get calls from buyers wanting to see a house, calls from people responding to your marketing, and the next thing you know you've missed your prospecting time. If you create a schedule and dedicate yourself to following it at least 75% of the time, your production will soar.

- To build an effective schedule, outline every single place you need to be and what you need to do for the next 30-60 days. Input personal events such as school functions, family events, time with your significant other, etc. This is important so that your personal commitments don't collide with your business life.
- Next list your business commitments. Include coaching time, programs, networking events, continued education, training classes, or meeting with your accountant, for example.
- Number three, put your prospecting time in your plan. Set time blocks in your schedule for the time you work on getting more listings into your plan. Stick to them as closely as you can.
- An important thing to factor into your plan is a time to work on your skills. I think now more than ever, building your skill set is important because you're going to be competing with so many different people within the same market. Set yourself apart.

Focus on your profitable activities

At the end of the day, there are only two things you do to be profitable: you either talk to buyers or you talk to sellers.

- Set standards for your business with your lifestyle in mind. I personally am not a great buyer's agent, as I don't work well while at the mercy of other people's schedules. If you're working with sellers and your business is more listing-heavy, you can control your time. You can leverage your time with listings, which you just can't do with buyers. Personally, I'll only work with a buyer if it's a friend, a family member, a past client, or a direct referral from one of those three. On top of that, you absolutely need to have a qualification process that you need to walk every buyer lead through.
- Questions you should prepare include: who they are, where they're from, what they want, when they're looking to purchase, where they want to be, their price range, and how they're going to pay for it. Essentially, the who, what, when, where, and how.
- Showing services are a great way to handle your listings in a way that notifies your sellers when someone wants to see the property, and all you have to do is put up the listing. If agents are looking to transition into listing-heavy business, I recommend they start looking for a buyer's agent that's organized and trustworthy, with a referral basis.

Focus on your forgotten lead sources

Seek out predictable lead sources and work these sellers through your process, add them to your database, and employ a full follow-up system. You need to have a replicable system that every client goes through and follow the same scripts over and over again.

- One of the most overlooked sources are For Rent by Owners. Call, inquire about the property, and whether they're looking to sell in the future. The key is to send a pre-listing package and follow up each month. Two key factors to know about For Rents: 1) the lease will end; and 2) nobody wants to deal with a bad tenant. Any of these owners could be simply one bad tenant away from putting the place on the market.

- Pre-foreclosure properties are another forgotten lead source. They can be located through your local courthouse or online services. I like RedX for going through FSBO's, expireds, and pre-foreclosures. Even your local Craigslist could have some good leads to explore. Send anyone selling a property an email asking for a contact number. You won't believe how easy it is because if their number isn't on the listing, nobody else is calling.

- One thing I like to do is drive around the neighborhood looking for For Sale by Owner signs that are put up on lawns that are maybe faded. That's a fantastic way to get leads.

- Lastly, newspapers. People don't look at local newspapers as often as they used to, but the classifieds are still a great resource for local properties. It's a little extra work, but it's worth it because nobody else is going for them in your market.

Final Thoughts for Success

Get in touch with people who are *connectors*—people who have a large sphere of influence and who will send people your way. Most importantly, *always* identify yourself as an agent. We're in a business nowadays where trust is the only thing we have. Be upfront with your intentions when you meet with them. In the end, it's all about building that trust.

Think outside the box and utilize strong communication skills to find leads and position yourself as the expert. Practice reading scripts with friends or family, and role play situations and answers for any questions that come up. It's important to flex your brain, because just like working out, you get better at it over time. Just keep going and keep at it, and success will follow.

"Think outside the box and utilize strong communication skills to find leads and position yourself as the expert."

Jason Morris

Chelsea Peitz

is a nationally recognized real estate keynote speaker who teaches camera-first branding strategies and is the creator of "Chelschat Marketing Snappily Ever After," the first real estate education daily show on Snapchat.

She is the President and Co-Founder of **TheAgentMarketer.com**, the only comprehensive online university for real estate and mortgage professionals for digital branding, social media and internet marketing. Chelsea is also the published author of the book, *Talking in Pictures*, the only book about how camera-first social platforms have changed how we build a personal brand. A frequent podcast and live stream guest, Chelsea shares actionable insights and tactics to help agents develop a powerful personal brand: https://www.theagentmarketer.com.

She is a national social selling coach who has developed one of the only curricula focused on using social platforms.

"As a national speaker, I share how camera-first platforms like Snapchat and live social video are critical to reaching modern consumers, how to communicate authentically and story tell, not story-sell."

- #1 Real Estate Snapchatter in the U.S. - *Inman News*
- Featured in the *Huffington Post*
- Listed as one of the "Top 10 People Dominating the Real Estate Industry on Snapchat" in 2016

Chapter 5

Creating a Camera-First Brand Strategy

Chances are, you've heard the buzz about Snapchat! However, most adults have no idea how to even use the app let alone create any sort of brand strategy with it.

My name is Chelsea Pietz, and I'm here to educate you on the possibilities of using Snapchat to boost your business. I am the author of *Talking in Pictures: How Snapchat Changed Cameras, Communication and Communities*.

I have more than 16 years of experience with real estate and currently serve as the Assistant VP and Director of Social Strategy for Fidelity National Title. I've been featured in the *Huffington Post*, *Inman News* and Inman Connect. I'm also the creator of "Chelschat" Snapshow: Marketing Snappily Ever After, a weekday Snapchat series sharing real estate marketing tips, tools and strategies.

I want you to know that Snapchat is not just for kids anymore! Today, the fastest growing population of Snapchat users are 40-year-old women. Snapchat is a fun way to create a camera-first brand strategy, and I can't wait to share it with you.

I will bring you into my world of Snapchat, and unveil for you how using Snapchat daily is not only fun and entertaining, but big business.

Some of the things you will learn include:
- Why Snapchat changed all social media and branding
- How to use it to build a brand and grow an engaged community of followers
- What the best content practices are with utilizing Snapchat

First off, I want to go over some statistics. These probably have grown even higher since the time I got these, but there are currently about 160 million daily users and over 2.5 billion snaps a day. Over 60% of users snap daily and visit eighteen times a day. What are the rest of the people doing? They're messaging. This is important, because Snapchat is a very message-driven app. Snapchat is about real-time visual communication and creating a community *through* the camera authentically. Images on Snapchat are based on talking, which is a great way to connect with people you don't know in a way where people expect you to start talking to them.

Snapchat users, on average, create more daily content than those on other social media platforms. Users are voluntarily engaging in advertisements. People are excited and delighted to open up a face line that may be sponsored or paid for by Gatorade or a local movie, and play with them and share them out to their community. You won't find that kind of engagement on any other platform other than Snapchat!

When it came out in 2011, Snapchat was mainly photos that disappeared. Then it became the precursor to live video. It became "Hey, I'm here at a party. You can be here with me too!" As Evan Spiegel, Snapchat CEO said, we went from the accumulation model of 'everything happening in the past' to instant expression, which is where social media is going. Everything is instant expression: on-demand and live.

What's so special about disappearing content? In essence, it's meant to mimic real life. Just like having a conversation or a coffee with a friend, once the time is done, without recordings, it's gone. That's the philosophy of Snapchat. Like a real-time conversation, it creates a sense of urgency. The 24-hour window to watch a story means that people know if they miss it, it's gone. That's why I got into Snapchat -- real time really is human time.

Like other messaging-based platforms, you don't have to know anybody's contact information to reach out to them on Snapchat. If they have an account, you can message them directly. That's one of the things that makes Snapchat such a powerhouse: being able to message someone directly and expect a reply. Right now, two and a half billion people have a messaging app installed on their phone and having an account on a message-based platform can help people connect with you more easily.

What Snapchat Brings to the Social Media Game

Snapchat has a three-pronged approach to engaging with your audience. The communication is real-time, which helps you build trust. The camera is another key ingredient. If you're not on camera in 2018, you will not exist. Whatever you may be is about what people see on camera. And then communities: super important. Creating communities equates to more private spaces where people can build their comfort and trust.

Snapchat hired a sociologist to hook people on the app and here's what they learned:

- **Habit-forming.** You use Snapchat once, and when you see good content on the app, it drives you to check in at a later time.
- **Mastery.** The layout is deliberately clunky and confusing for beginners, but it pushes its users to learn the ins and outs of the app and keeps them coming back for more. The more time you put into learning something, the more likely you are to keep using it.
- **Faces.** When you're using Snapchat, you're talking *to* the camera. You're actually engaging one-on-one with anyone who's watching you. Watching someone eye-to-eye every day creates a sense of trust that's so important in our industry.
- **Authenticity.** When you're on camera for so many hours, days, or months on end, you can't help but show the real side of you. Consumers want a face they can engage with and can respond immediately. The camera is the new social feed.

What Should I Be Posting on Snapchat?

Documenting your life through photos and live video is a great form of storytelling. Not by selling anything but by sharing what you do just by documenting. It really isn't a live stream. It's a life stream.

Your primary goal on Snapchat should be about building a relationship. It's about letting people know who you are and being relatable. That's one step towards building your brand and then generating leads. It's especially important for real-estate professionals, because our business is *built* on relationships. Our potential clients see us doing what we love and what we're passionate about. With a little work, you too can make Snapchat work for you and build some great relationships of your own!

"Documenting your life through photos and live video is a great form of storytelling."

Chelsea Peitz

Frank Patrick is

veteran of the real estate business and is currently licensed in the state of Arizona. Frank began his career in Missouri in 2000 at a small community just outside Kansas City. Within just a few years, Frank was the owner of a nationally-franchised real estate brokerage with 38 agents. Although the duties of broker/owner were considerable, Frank managed to average over  100 transaction sides a year for 14 years in a row. In 2007, Frank started his agent training business and has helped over 10,000 agents through his live webinar training programs. Today, Frank specializes in helping agents break into the lucrative Probate Listing niche. It is estimated that more than a million homeowners die each year without a fully vested trust. These homeowners leave behind property that must be sold to settle the estate. Before these houses can be listed and sold, they must pass through the Probate Court. Most agents have absolutely no idea how the process works or how to obtain these listings.

Chapter 6

Breaking Into the Probate Niche

What if you could look into the future and see who is going to list a house in your market area six months from now? Would that give you an unfair advantage over your competitors?

I'm Frank Patrick, a Real Estate Broker, and I'm going to teach you how to generate a steady stream of ready-to-sell listings by tapping into the little-known probate niche.

As a Probate Listing Expert, I will utilize my insider knowledge and expertise to show you how to get probate listings in your area.

As a real estate broker for nearly two decades, I have discovered that "you have to list to last." Developing a system to consistently list new properties each and every week should be your #1 priority. If you have listings, you can leverage them to generate buyer and seller leads for very little additional money or time. This greatly reduces your advertising expense and increases your profit margin. I've found that I can work with four times as many sellers as I can buyers. My business goal has always been to generate the greatest return on my time and money invested into my business. Over the years, I have met many "Top Producers" that sell hundreds of homes a year but barely eke out a modest profit. While it's nice to win awards and the admiration of our peers, you cannot deposit trophies into your bank account.

In my opinion, the greatest challenge that agents face today is choosing how to spend their time and money to get clients. I could list 100 or more ways to spend your advertising budget and all of them will generate leads. Unfortunately, most will not be profitable or sustainable in the long run. Most brokers and trainers will tell you that "everyone is a prospect." While this sounds good in theory the numbers prove otherwise. According to the US Census Bureau, there are approximately 87 million home owners in the US. The latest report by the National Association of Realtors shows there were roughly 5 million real estate transactions last year. Using these two numbers, we can quickly calculate that 6% of the 87 million homeowners completed a real estate transaction. That means that 94% of homeowners did not buy or sell. If you farm a neighborhood of 100 residences, the national average tells us that you can expect six of those homeowners to list and sell during the next 12 months. Therefore, the time, money and effort you spent marketing to the other 94 is wasted. But what if you could look into the future and see which six were going to sell? You could focus your effort on just those six and achieve greater results at a much lower cost.

The Probate Opportunity

It is estimated that over a million homeowners die each year without a fully vested trust. In the absence of a fully vested trust, the estate must go through Probate. This creates a public record and allows you to identify a prospect that is 90% likely to sell within 12 months. We've found that there is very little competition for these listings as most agents don't know how the process works or what they can do to obtain these listings.

41

The Numbers:

• 2.5 million people over the age of 30 die each year in the USA.
• 90% of people do not have a fully vested trust. No trust = Probate (if there are any debts or assets).
• 65% own at least one property.
• 90% will sell within 12 months.

What Is Probate?

Probate is the legal process through which the court oversees the estate of a deceased person to make sure the debts are paid and the estate is properly distributed to their heirs. Many people think probate applies to you only if you have a will. Not so! If you don't have a fully vested trust, your estate will be probated whether or not you have a will.

- **With a valid will:** Your will determines how your estate is transferred during probate and to whom.
- **Without a valid will:** The laws in the state where you live specify who gets which parts of your estate.
- Think of the probate process as the "map" that guides the orderly transfer of your estate according to the rules.

Why Probate?

- Leads can be obtained through public records
- 90% of leads sell within 12 months
- Inexpensive to market to the leads
- Little competition
- Other agents can't copy your marketing
- When you have inventory, you get buyers for free
- When you sell the listing, the heirs become buyer prospects
- It's not economically driven
- Once you figure it out, it can be scaled and much of the work can be outsourced or delegated
- No referral fees or high-cost client acquisition

The Five Secrets to Get Probate Listings:

1. **Probate leads.** There are several ways to obtain the leads. Probate cases require public notification. Therefore, you can obtain the leads from the courthouse, from legal publications, from online aggregators or from companies that sell probate leads. If you have more time to invest than money, you can get the leads for free. If you have more money than time, you can purchase the leads.

2. **Not all leads are equal.** It is estimated that 75% of all probate cases have real estate. You'll want to make sure you are only marketing to those prospects. You can search property tax records to determine if a case contains real estate. If you are buying leads, make sure they are scrubbing the list of cases that do not contain real estate in your market area.

3. **Marketing to probate leads.** We send a series of "lumpy" direct mail packages to the person in charge of the disposition of the estate. This person is the executor, personal representative, or administrator of the estate. We have had the best result by sending a series of four letters each, 30 days apart. We mail, then follow up with a "warm call" after the letter, and repeat for a total of four letters and four calls. We send the first letter when we receive the lead, and then letter two in thirty days, letter three at 60 days and letter four at 90 days. The letters are written to build rapport, establish authority and create reciprocity in the mind of the prospect.

4. **What you mail is important.** Our first letter is an introduction that positions me as a specialist in Probate Real Estate. For that first mailing, I do not ask for the listing, instead I offer to be a resource should they have questions. The envelope is addressed by hand and I

include a ball point pen (creates the lump in the envelope and has a special message imprinted). The second letter informs them that I can refer them to a competent locksmith, lawn care company, handyman, probate attorney, etc., should they need assistance. The third letter informs them that I can help them if they want to sell the property quickly, as is, to an all-cash buyer, or I can help them get full-market value. The fourth letter offers them a free CMA to help them determine the value of the property. All four direct mail pieces contain a free item of value chosen to create a lump in the envelope and further build rapport, authority and reciprocity. This gets the letters opened and makes each call a "warm call." We spend an average of $18 to acquire and mail to each lead. Our goal is to list 6% of the leads in our pipeline. With an average commission of $9,000 in my marketplace, the return on investment is very high. If we spend $1,800 to mail a series of four letters to 100 leads, we expect to list six properties and earn a total of $54,000 in Gross Commission Income. That's a 30 to 1 return. In other words, we spend $1 to make $30.

5. **If you call after each letter you will double your success.** We only find telephone numbers for about 50% of the prospects. If you have the number, use it. Simply call to see if they received the letter, ask if they have any questions for you, tell them they can call you any time. My motto is "Service Before Self Interest".

For more information on how to get Probate Listings go to:
www.HowToGetProbateListings.com

"Identify the 6% that are going to sell and only spend your time, money and energy marketing to them, it is that simple."

Frank Patrick

John Reh has been a licensed Realtor since 2011 and started using Facebook Advertising that same year. He's also the Director of Facebook Strategy for the 150-agent brokerage where he works at in Chicago.

John combines years of real estate knowledge, business ownership experience, and relevant education (MBA Marketing, Certified Facebook Ads Account Manager), to effectively teach Realtors and Mortgage Professionals how to use the amazing Facebook platform to grow their businesses.

Certified Facebook Ads Account Manager

john@socialtippingpoint.com

Website: http://socialtippingpoint.com/

Facebook Page with free weekly live training:

https://www.facebook.com/SocialTippingPoint/

Chapter 7

The Exact Blueprint On How to Use Facebook Advertising

Are you looking to tap into Facebook Advertising? If you're like most agents, you know you should be using Facebook in your business, but you just don't know how (yet).

I'm John Reh of Social Tipping Point, and I'll lay out for you the exact blueprint on how to use Facebook Advertising to make this your best year ever! I have been a full-time Realtor in Chicago since 2011 and have been using Facebook Advertising that entire time. I'm also the Facebook Strategy Director for a 150-agent brokerage and have helped agents at all skill levels understand and use Facebook Advertising for real estate through my training and support community, Social Tipping Point, which you can find on Facebook.

In this section, I'll cover methods such as:

- The easiest and quickest way to get the biggest bang for your buck with Facebook
- How to use Facebook Ads even if you're a complete Facebook "newbie"

- The only four things a busy agent really needs to do with Facebook
- How to dominate any hyper-local market for just $1 per day
- The #1 thing Facebook does NOT want you to do
- As an added bonus, I am going to break down my #1 seller lead generation ad that my brokerage is using to get seller leads for roughly $5 each, so that you can copy and use it for yourself

Now is the time to be planning for the year, and by using the most powerful advertising platform ever conceived (Facebook), I'll show you how to reach your goals. So, let's get started.

Now, with websites like Zillow, Trulia, and even our own industry associations, it can be increasingly hard for agents like us to know when and where our next clients are coming from as their methods try to disrupt the real estate industry one way or another.

The good thing is, we have a way to fight back: Your best defense is to use Facebook as your personal stage to show thousands of people that *you* are the only possible person that they can trust. By doing this, you create relationships where these websites can't. As real estate agents, the best tool we have is our ability to create relationships with our clients.

Why is Facebook so powerful? Never has there been a platform as smart, or that learns as quickly. The amount of information it knows about us is staggering and you can use this to your advantage.

The first thing you'll need to do is forget what you know about "old" social media rules. That's right: free posts are dead. That's fine though because, with the new ways you can use Facebook, you can spend a minimal amount of money (even just $100 a month) and get your posts in front of *thousands* of new eyeballs and see how many people engage with your content through Facebook analytics.

We can compare this to what we know in real estate. Think of Facebook like direct mail: what if you could send out 4,000 postcards and know which 50 people hung them on their fridge with a magnet? That's exactly what Facebook does. Then, what you can do is send those same 50 people more content to let them get to know you and establish their trust. Facebook can be daunting, but here are the four simple steps you're going to need to focus on.

Post Your Activity

You're going to need a Facebook business page (not a personal page) to run ads on. Once you have that, the first basic action to take is to broadcast your activity and show people that you're active in real estate. Do this over and over again to people who already know you as well as to the areas where you want people to get to know you, and soon enough, people will connect with your passion. Establish yourself in the community as an expert, and the trust will follow. Other activities you can do include posting your available listings and see who clicks on them. From there, you can create custom audiences, which basically means that you can track a "bucket" of people that took a certain action, and you can send them more information and get them engaged in your content.

Target People You Already Know

Upload your contact list to Facebook. This is an easy way to first connect with the people you already know. Facebook is going to match people that are in your customer file with those who have a Facebook account. That way, you don't have to invite them one by one to like your page, but you can still send them content.

Now, don't be *that* guy who just takes contact information and provides nothing in return. Facebook *hates* that, and could shut you down very quickly if you're continually offering a bad user experience. Remember to provide value to your clients, and they'll be good to you.

Digital Farming: Create Custom Audiences

Digital farming is the exact same concept we work on in real estate with geographic targeting, but online. If you want to target a town, neighborhood, or local area, this is how you do it. You can easily target a geographic area that's valuable to you and gradually grow your audience and your credibility in that area to know exactly where your leads are coming from.

You can do this for as little as one dollar per day with a hyper-local area like a subdivision or neighborhood. For example, take a short video walkthrough of a listing or a testimonial of someone whose house you just sold in an area, and run it for a month. And that will put you in front of all the people in that neighborhood. If you've been creating quality content for them, then over time you'll have a huge gathering of people that have seen you in these videos for months on end, and you've provided value to them over and over again. Who do you think they're going to call when they're ready? It's going to be you, the expert they've been seeing for the past few months every three days on Facebook.

Utilize Retargeting

Using the audiences you've built from watching your content and other activity, you can then customize your posts to retarget the people you think will engage with them the most. People looking to sell their homes, for example, might engage with a home valuation ad. People looking to buy will be the ones that click through your listings. Over time, you'll learn to play around with these audiences and learn which ones are the most cost-effective for you.

If you're wondering "How do I get new leads?", we'll need new audiences, a larger geographic space, and valuable content to create tangible leads. The number one ad we run for sellers is our home valuation ad. By offering a home valuation (preferably with an automated valuation service), I guarantee you *will* get leads. Place your website and contact information in the ad and you can start building relationships and get a head start on other agents by gathering information. If you know what you're doing, you can cut down on lead generation costs very quickly. Also, be as specific as you can in your ads to localize your audience as much as you can.

Remember -- targeting never overcomes a weak message or offer. 99% of the time, if you're not getting the results you wanted, it's the message, not the platform. This is still advertising and you need to have a powerful message that connects with people first.

This is really all you need to do, and no other platform can do it like Facebook. Ultimately, be a good person. Deliver value. Build trust, and you'll build clients. You may have noticed that this is exactly how business is done in real life except that, through Facebook, we get to speed up the process and do it on a mass scale instead of one by one.

"You may have noticed that this is exactly how business is done in real life except that, through Facebook, we get to speed up the process and do it on a mass scale instead of one by one."

John Reh

Hoss Pratt is a nationally known authority on lead generation and lead conversion. He has demonstrated time and time again during his stellar career that using his revolutionary strategies can move brokers and agents from stuck to super charged in just months… all the while improving lives and changing fortunes.

Hoss Pratt is the CEO and founder of Hoss Pratt Success Systems, the premier resource for agents and firms that want to take their business to the next level. This renowned coaching and training firm helps client's build better real estate businesses.

Chapter 8

How to Go from 0-30 Listings in 30 Days

I'm Hoss Pratt, the #1 Real Estate 'Sales & Marketing' Coach, and what I will share with you is guaranteed to change the way you do real estate! I'm a National Real Estate Coach and Trainer, author of the best-selling book *Listing Boss: The Definitive Blueprint for Real Estate Success,* and Founder and CEO of Success Systems.

If you're a professional who's serious about building a lucrative real estate empire, this content-rich training is just for you.

I'll provide you with the exact blueprint to:

- Bring in an avalanche of new listings by tapping the MOST NEGLECTED target markets.
- Build a VIRTUAL listing machine that gushes profits.
- Get your prospects to say "YES" with these four easy strategies.
- Go from ZERO business to over 30 homes a month… every month!

My first six months in real estate were absolutely brutal. I was a farm boy from Missouri, 21-years old, working 80 hours a week without a single listing or buyer in those six months. And I blew through $50, 000. I either had to change what I was doing, or I had to move back to Missouri. And I went from that to 30 listings in the next t30 days by following the path I'm about to lay out for you.

Four Pillars of Success

This is something that that I've learned not only from my own experience, but from helping other people in real estate over the course of the last twelve years.

Mindset

Mindset is *everything* in real estate. The reason I was broke those first six months was because I thought I was like every other real estate agent. If you're not happy where you are financially in your business today, it's the direct result of your actions from the last six months. If that's you, you have to change *today.* Get out of your comfort zone and look inward for success, not outward.

Marketing

I want you to think of yourself as a marketer who just happens to be in real estate and I want you to ask yourself one question: Why should your prospects use you instead of your competitor? Now I want you to remember this: people don't really care about you. They care about themselves, their time, and their money. They care about how *you're* going to help *them.*

You'll need a solid marketing arsenal if you're going to convince prospects you're the person for the job. Have a performance guarantee, a communication guarantee, a risk-free offer, a Smart Seller Program, a Marketing plan -- things that set you apart from everybody else.

Create an Easy Exit Listing to make it easy for your prospects to use you, and give people a risk-free out if they don't want to be locked into a contract. The amount of business you gain from this offer far exceeds the amount of business that you lose by using it.

Now, the single biggest complaint about realtors is the lack of communication. This is where the communication guarantee comes into play. Talk to your sellers on a set schedule, and guarantee them their communication time.

The Smart Seller Program is something that allows the seller to sell the property themselves while it's listed with me. If they sell it, I don't get a commission. This gets a *lot* of people to say "yes" to you that otherwise wouldn't have. The SSP also comes with a menu of commission rates that gives your sellers options, and gives them a lot of flexibility that can tip the scales in your favor when they pick out an agent.

Be aggressive and specific in your marketing plan. Sellers want an agent who has a plan, and can tell them specifically how they're getting their property sold. Which sounds better? "I've been in business for 30 years" or "I've been to 5,767 successful closings"? This marketing is paramount to your success.

Systems

I want you to diversify your systems. Don't rely on one system, one tool, one relationship, one builder, one referral source or one business source. Have multiple lines in multiple niches.

The fastest ways to get listings, bar none, are FSBO's, Expired, Distress, Probate, and SOI: Sphere of Influence. I love niches where 100% of the niche are selling their homes. All you have to do is put your marketing in front of them and see who says "yes."

Here are the tools you'll want. First, you want a Customer Relations Management (CRM) software. I need you to depend on that CRM like a lifeline, and remember, the best CRM is the one that you use.

You also need a lead provider. My preferred lead provider is Landvoice, a website that sends you all the FSBOs, Expireds, and all the other information every day.

To receive a special discount on leads, go here: www.landvoice.com/hoss

An important point when dealing with FSBO's is that you must genuinely want the FSBO to sell their property on their own and ask for the opportunity to *earn* their business if they don't. If you go at it any other way, it's a surefire way to lock yourself out of the niche. Be in touch, communicate, and be the agent that's ready when they're ready to throw in the towel. Have a follow-up system that runs over months to keep in touch with that seller that tells why they should do business with you.

Conversion
This is where the rubber hits the road. At the end of the day, if you don't convert those leads you're getting, you're just spinning your wheels. It'll take only two weeks for you to build momentum, but I'm going to need you to commit to those two weeks. Ask yourself: *Is what I'm doing right now a money-making activity?* In real estate, it's up to *you* to get out there and make that money.

Three Questions to Ask at First Contact
You've got to get really good at selecting who is worth your time and money if you're going to get anywhere. There are three questions I use to go through all the FSBO's to determine exactly this.

- If I brought you a qualified buyer, would you be willing to pay a 3% co-op?
- How long are you going to try to sell the property on your own before you decide to explore other options?

- In that time frame, if you decide to explore other options, would you be open to interviewing some more aggressive agents?

4 Steps to the "Yes"
- **Be Direct.** You need people to see your confidence and your vibe to get them to say "yes" to you. When you're in a conversation, you're in charge, not them.
- **Pattern Interrupt.** Most people aren't actively looking to talk to a realtor. Break their pattern and start asking questions before they hang up on you. We want people to be open to talking to us.
- **Dig Deep.** Ask a question, wait for them to answer, and ask another question based on that answer. You want to go at *least* three levels deep. Find the problem and offer a solution.
- **Voice Control.** Show your energy through your voice. Energy will remove *all* doubt. Enthusiasm is the single most powerful ingredient in communication. Get fired up!

These are all things you can do *today* to extract the maximum result in the precious time you invest in real estate and get you and your business to where you want to be.

Get a copy of my #1 International Best-Selling Book **"Listing Boss:** *The Definitive Blueprint For Real Estate Success***"**. Visit www.ListingBossBook.com and I'll send you a copy!

"The best CRM is the one that you use."

Hoss Pratt

Chris Johnstone is the CEO of Connection Inc.

www.connectionincorporated.com

They provide digital marketing solutions for mortgage lenders that drive quality leads and ROI. If you are looking for quality, reliable lead generation from Google or Facebook, head over to their website and book a free strategy call.

Chapter 9

Target Ads by Email Addresses in Adwords

I am Chris Johnstone, and I am here to help you understand exactly how to use Google's valuable tool, Adwords.

For the first time ever, Google has introduced "Customer Match" where you can upload your customers and promotional email lists to Adwords and target those in list in the Adwords. Targeting custom audiences by uploading email marketing lists is a powerful tool used by Twitter and Facebook Advertisers.

The new Customer Match feature of Google is its answer to Facebook's "Custom Audience" ad targeting feature. Facebook lets brands target people based on their email ID, phone numbers, user IDs and mobile ad IDs, whereas Google lets brands target people based on only their email addresses.

The Customer Match feature of Google Adwords will help you to reach the highest value customers on Google Search, YouTube and Gmail. Through Customer Match, you can build campaigns which are specifically designed to reach your audience.

Google's Customer Match helps you to:
- Create awareness among the customers who are more likely to be interested in your product
- Make tailor-made marketing campaigns targeting specific audiences
- Improve purchase through upselling and cross-sell strategies
- Promotes repeated purchase and increases loyalty

Unlike Facebook, Google Adwords is based on targeting your past customers -- meaning you'll ideally already have your customers' trust before you begin your campaign. Your goal is to get them to do business with you *again,* or to have them refer you to their business partners or peers. If you're actively running an ad campaign on Facebook or Google, you should *absolutely* be running retargeting as well.

The ads that you want to run can be any of the following:
- **Success stories from a past client.** Remember to be punchy and direct with your text here: simple things to drive people to click on that ad.
- **Branding.** A little reminder of you and your brand so that you're at the top of your client's mind when they need a name for a referral.
- **Testimonials.** This can be when somebody has left a direct review on your page or your business profile or your website. Take the text from the review and turn it into an ad on the network.

Next, you'll want a call to action. Ask people to call you with real estate questions and be sure that your phone number is visible in the advertisement! These lead to different types of results. You can put any contact information in your ads, such as your email addresses, or through Direct Messages, and even via webforms that make it easy for people to contact you.

Now, about conversion mechanisms! We've found that clicks can be converted into the amount of traffic an ad drives to your website, whether or not someone fills out a form, or refers a friend to your page, but the *primary* conversion mechanism we've had is people calling the number on our ads. These are people who just ring up the number and say "Hey, I saw you on Google. Could you help with this?" And that right there is a great advertisement.

Here's the beautiful thing about retargeting. Retargeting brings you the highest quality leads—in many cases—that you've already paid for. That can be practically double the amount of leads at a fraction of the cost of the original campaign. When you do business with somebody, that is *not* the end of your lifetime customer relationship with that client. When you generate that first deal, it's the *start* of the relationship with that person. And retargeting puts you right back in front of those customers.

We've all been through that experience where we look on a website, maybe Amazon or something else, and you bounce without filling anything in or going through with a purchase. Suddenly when you go onto other websites, you see other ads for that same product. *That's* retargeting. Keeping the product fresh in your mind and right in front of your face. The best part is it's also one of the easiest to get into digital marketing systems available today. For just a little more than five dollars a day, you could be bringing your brand presence into that same marketplace. That kind of quality retargeting can convert "lost" leads off your website from people who didn't opt in, generate more referrals from your past customers, and can build you an *incredible* brand presence in your local space.

First off, set up an account at adwords.google.com. Then, give Google the audience by simply pressing a button under 'Shared Libraries' that says, "Remarketing List." You can then create audiences that span from your website visitors, mobile app users, and every customer that you've ever done business with. Also remember to remove demographic, location, and other limitations from the campaign settings so you can cast your net as wide as you possibly can.

Little tip: You want to set the expiration for the ad campaign to 120 days, just so you don't inundate people with these advertisements. Normally, 120 days is more than enough to get a response. Keep renewing your audience within Adwords at least once a quarter to keep those names fresh.

I have to be clear here. There *has* to be express consent from the customer here: customers who have said "Yes, send me updates and future communication," from the people in this list in order for you to use this tool. If you have older clients that you haven't contacted in a while, feel free to reach out to them and ask them if they'd like to opt into your new campaigns. It reminds them of your presence and -- if they say yes -- could lead to return business and quality referrals you'd miss on otherwise.

Now, there are different kinds of ad campaigns you can run. You have your search ads that come up at the top when you do a Google search, Gmail ads, and Youtube ads. Pick the ad that you want your retargeting campaign to run on. For Gmail ads, you'll have to specify that you want to run your campaign *only* on mail.google.com, which is what brings the cost down significantly. With the rest of the ads you want to run, there's only one caveat -- whatever websites you'll want to run ads on has to be part of the Google AdSense network, which over 70% of the websites online already are, especially the major ones you'll already be targeting.

One more thing: *follow up* with your clients. The worst thing you can do with a lead generated from your ad campaign is forget about them. Have an automatic sequence that can contact people who have opted in when something they've tagged is listed. Send them an initial email and a reminder. This sequence can run for 30 days and *then* place them into a long-term nurture sequence. It takes people an average of 90 days to go from 'maybe we can buy a house,' get their finances in order, and then come back and seriously go through the process of finding their perfect house. If you have that automatic sequence in place, you'll be at the front of their mind when they're finally ready to dive in and commit to buying their new home.

"The worst thing you can do with a lead generated from your ad campaign is forget about them."

Chris Johnstone

Enrique Braunschweiger is the President and Founder of First West Financial in La Quinta California. He has over 15 years of experience originating loans and has over 1 Billion dollars in funded transactions. Enrique has built a solid Mortgage company that focuses on serving the community, but also supports the success of his Real Estate partners.

With a background in the hospitality and vacation business, Enrique made the leap to the Mortgage Industry with one thing in mind, helping people become homeowners and supporting the efforts of those agents that share the same goal. Enrique uses a unique approach to grow his business, he calls it the 4 E's for Mortgage success.

1- **Education**, investing and sharing new and useful information to buyers and agents alike
2- **Empowerment**, giving people the tools and guidance to become homeowners and giving agents the necessary guidance to help others
3- **Engagement**, reaching out to the real estate community and also to the general public especially underserved sectors of our society such as First Time Buyers, Veterans and minorities, etc.
4- **Execution**, taking action, taking ideas and making them a reality.

Enrique is a devoted husband of 24 years, his wife and partner Kris is the co-owner of First West Financial, and as a team they have built a great company and an amazing family.

Enrique is active in his church and community, he is the father of two, his son Austin is an accounting analyst in Los Angeles and his daughter Alex is a Junior in high school.

Chapter 10

First-Time Buyer Boot Camp for Agents

How do you lower the risk and maximize your chances with first-time buyers?

I'm Enrique Braunschweiger and I am the owner of First West Financial in Southern California. I have funded close to one billion dollars in real estate transactions and 70% of them are first-time buyers! This is incredible because statistically, first-time buyers go through three different agents before settling with a fourth agent that will actually sell them a home.

According to real estate statistics, this year 45% of all transactions in the US will involve a first-time buyer. If you are not an expert at this, you are missing out on a great opportunity!

I am a loan officer and real estate broker and would love to share what I have learned in over 15 years in this segment of the real estate market. I will teach you four simple, yet effective and duplicable techniques that will help you increase your ability to attract, execute and retain all of your first-time buyer prospects that you choose to work with.

The Psychology of the First Time Buyer (FTB)

There are some things you'll need to know if you're dealing with FTB's. They're scared, indecisive, confused and—most importantly—either over-informed or misinformed altogether. In order to overcome those issues, you must position yourself as an advisor. They need to understand that you're there to give them advice. You're the expert, a friendly figure, trusted professional, competent, and *you're* the person they want to do business with.

Tools of the Trade

Here's the reality: most first time buyers get their agents from someone they know. The number one source you'll have for first time buyers isn't going to be the internet—it's going to be someone who told them about you.

Two valuable tools to assist you in this are social media and a Customer Relationship Management (CRM) tool. This customer database automates outgoing communication, sets reminders for follow-ups, and keeps a consistent log of all the communication between you and a prospect. There are dozens of options out there that are available and easily found on the Internet, but the best CRM you can have will *always* be the one you use.

Big question here: on a yearly basis how many times are you supposed to touch a past client or sphere of influence person? Here's the number: 24. I recommend one email per month that's not real estate-related, four phone calls a year (once per quarter, just to say "Hi"), four handwritten letters a year, and finally, four real-estate pieces: a flyer card, magnet or something you just sold. Stay in front of them, and when they're ready to buy, you're the one they call. If you're not mining your database and getting those referrals for first-time buyers, then somebody else is.

Social Media Marketing

Having a social media marketing plan is the simplest thing you can do for your business today. Start simple! Post your listings or invite people to contact you if they're looking to buy or sell. Always, always have a call to action.

You may even consider Facebook paid advertising. Facebook is something that you want to do consistently, and is geared towards first time buyers. It also works *wonders* with friends, families, and your sphere of influence.

With social media, content is key. Have at least 60% real-estate driven posts on your personal page. Every two weeks, put up a buyer-specific post with a call to action: a picture of a house, or a listing, and invite people to give you a call. Then, send a message to forty of your friends, top to bottom, and ask them to share it on their feeds. Realistically, probably only 40% will, but then your post will be out there to thousands of people who would have missed that post otherwise.

First Time Buyers

Once you get them, what do you do? First off, engage in a conversation. Be open with them, and explain your process so they know what to expect.

Next, send them a First Time Buyer Guide and ask questions. This short document provides information that the buyer might not know to simply and walk them through the process.

Also, take this opportunity to ask them questions. Is your buyer currently working with another agent? How long have they been looking for a home? Have they been pre-qualified? What area are they looking for? What size home?

You'd be amazed how little thought some people have given to these questions. Asking questions will build rapport and establish your authority. Asking questions tells the buyer that you care.

Tell them a lender is going to call them to get them pre-qualified and follow up and ask them if they have questions after reading the guide. After the call, follow up with your buyer to set up an appointment to flesh out details. Be sure to follow up with them consistently so that they know you're the agent to call.

Tools to Retain the Potential Buyer

- **Give them a loan calculator.** Preferably one that's not connected to any other real estate agent or companies. Give them something that's just a loan calculator with only you in it.
- **Set them up with a portal.** Set this up so that your buyer can search for homes, otherwise they'll find listings somewhere else.
- **Explain how Zillow and other sites work**. Explain to them that the realtors they see on the websites may not be the one selling the property they're looking at. Push the value of your trusted interactions.
- **Explain that some sites are not accurate or reputable.** Prevent your client from getting scammed on the internet.
- **Explain that you can sell them *any home.***
- **Tell them to call you or text you if they see a home they like *anywhere.***
- **The lender should call every Friday and see how the house hunting is going**. This is how you find out if they're cheating on you. Call them every Friday and you could save a lot of potential deals.
- **Follow up, follow up, and follow up.**

Your 90-Day Action Plan

Your next 90 days could be the ones that change your life and your business.

- Implement a CRM with your past client database.
- Implement a 24-touch program to your existing database.
- Start posting on social media with calls to action.
- Create a customized First Time Buyer Guide.
- Meet with your lender and ask him for support.

These simple steps are all you need to become an expert at closing those first-time buyer deals. And it could all start today!

Download your first-time home buyers guide using this link: http://bit.ly/firsttimebuyersguide

"If you're not mining your database and getting those referrals for first-time buyers, then somebody else is."

Enrique Braunschweiger

Erin Bradley is a wife and a mom, a coach, and a successful entrepreneur, who brings a contagious enthusiasm to every endeavor. Her zest for life and love of adventure led her to forego the steady paycheck of a salaried job in 2007 to pursue the "freedom and flexibility" of self-employment in the mortgage industry. It didn't take long for her to realize that being your own boss isn't always as romantic as it sounds!

As her bank account suffered early on, Erin became passionate about the disconnect between doing what you love, and financial freedom. She's been on a mission ever since to bridge that gap for herself and everyone she meets. Over the years, Erin has developed a simple, yet effective, system to help fellow entrepreneurs overcome the fear of sales, and promote their business in a way that feels natural and easy. She shares her strategy through candid and often comical stories, in an effort to inspire others to never give up, and pursue the life of *their* dreams.

Chapter 11

Creating The Life That You Are Meant To Live

What if there was a simple strategy that would allow you to be yourself, increase your referrals and have more fun growing your business?

I'm Erin Bradley, Loan Officer and bestselling author of the book _Pursuing Freedom_. I started in the mortgage business in 2006, and went 100% commission income in 2007. By 2008, I was so broke, I had to ride my bike to a first-time client meeting because I didn't have enough money for gas. When my credit card was declined for a small coffee, as the client walked in (and paid for my coffee), I was sure I'd hit rock bottom. I knew something had to give.

Born to Serve, Not Sell

Here's the thing: most entrepreneurs become self-employed because they're passionate about serving others, and they love their craft, not necessarily because we are born "salespeople." We know we need to communicate our value in order to survive, but making "sales calls" often feels self-serving, so we do nothing… and we struggle. After hitting my version of financial rock bottom, I went on a mission to find a solution, for myself and every entrepreneur I meet.

The problem I discovered with real estate and mortgage, is that most of our clients only need our services every couple of years, yet we need to stay top of mind. The traditional advice is to call people regularly and say, "If you know someone who needs a realtor/lender, I'm your guy." And frankly, I found this strategy challenging, because it focused on what I needed to *get,* instead of what I could *give.* I needed to find a way to provide value above and beyond doing their mortgage, in order to feel sincere about reaching out to begin with. So, I went about developing a detailed system for communicating with my target market, in an effort to solve *all* of their problems. That way, when the opportunity arose to hire me (or refer me), I was top of mind. The result was that my friends and family started thinking of me when they needed *anything.* I became a trusted resource to my clients/friends, and a referral source to my colleagues. Then, when both clients *and* colleagues needed a loan, or knew someone who did, they'd think of me, a thoughtful person, rather than a great salesperson. Make sense? Read below for your roadmap to more referrals!

Level 1 - Create Your Village and Your Tribe
THE "WHO" = THE "VILLAGE"

Figure out who you want to serve, and build your database. I refer to these people as my "Village." These should be people you genuinely like and want to serve. This should include friends, family, past clients, neighbors, coworkers, etc. Just look at your Facebook account -- you know a lot of people who deserve your level of service!
THE "HOW" = THE "TRIBE"

My goal is to serve my Village above and beyond what I get paid to do (which is close loans). I am on a mission to support them on their journey, and as a result, am top-of-mind when they (or someone they know) needs a loan. Build a directory of local businesses who can help your Village in every capacity. This includes everything from financial services, to home contractors, to health and wellness. This will be known as your Tribe.

To get started, print up a physical list of occupations where you can fill in the blanks. Think outside the box. People moving to a new area will need a new pediatrician, hairstylist, handyman, lawn care professional, dentist, etc. Everyone needs a financial planner, insurance agent and accountant. Become the referral directory! If you want to put an hour into sales and are having trouble asking for referrals, now you have a new purpose. Change the conversation, and ask your friends and family for referrals for local service providers. Leverage your Village to build your Tribe. This is how you get into 'activity' and on purpose, grow your business!

While on the phone, take it to the next level, and find out what's happening in your Village. Engagements, new babies, graduations, sickness, puppies... LIFE is always happening, and there's always a call to action! Instead of calling to make a sale, call to find out what is happening in your clients' and friends' lives. Once you start operating from passion and the heart, you operate on a more magnetic level. Your intention will shift to solving problems and helping people. Uncover their issues and solve them if you can, refer them if you can't. Connect them with your "Tribe" of trusted professionals.

To learn about clients, utilize the FROG system = Family, Recreation, Occupation and Goals. Ask questions in the categories such as "What fun things are you doing this weekend?," "Are you traveling for the holiday?," "Which team are you cheering for in the big game?" As soon as you find an action item, such as "My son just got into Bucknell," you send a Bucknell mug or baseball hat, and a handwritten note. Also, keep a pulse on social media to see what is happening in your clients' lives. Remember, the real estate closings are just one aspect of their lives. We need to be a resource in ALL areas of their lives!

Level Two -- Add the Tribe to Your Village

When I started out, a realtor friend and I gave business card binders to our clients with the professionals we could trust. We then worked with these professionals over coffee and coached them on how they could refer us as well and add even more value for their clients.

Getting in touch with these professionals isn't hard, as you have a warm lead. For example, you can say, "I have a client who said that you were an amazing dentist, and I need someone to refer my new clients to. Can we meet for coffee? I'd love to learn more about your business, and see how I can help you." It's that simple.

Just like with your Village, when meeting the business owners you've been referred to, you FROG, then resolve. Be a resource to *everyone you meet!* You're always growing your Tribe, and helping these professionals grow their business along the way.

Level 3 -- Marketing

You want to market in ways that no one else is. I knew that a monthly touch was important, so I began mailing a new introduction to a professional with their business card every month, which left my clients intrigued. At business events I made sure to connect people who could help each other by offering services, and we offered clients the business card binder of professionals at closing.

In addition to referrals, I teamed up with professionals to cross-promote. For example, I worked with a family photographer and provided a gift card for her services for a family photo shoot in my client's new home. They became a client of hers as well, and she continued to refer new business my way. This happened time and again. I can't encourage you enough to leverage your tribe and increase value.

Sales Calls Now Feel Like Service Calls

Now you know my secret to fooling myself into getting my sales calls done without them feeling like sales calls. My calls feel better because I have a mission and a purpose -- it is to fill in my list and to serve.

To go deeper with this Village and Tribe process and view my other helpful resources, please visit www.PursuingFreedom.com or find *Pursuing Freedom* on Amazon.

"You want to market in ways that no one else is."

Erin Bradley

COACH —
HANK
— AVINK

Hank Avink is a man of action and results. He was a millionaire by age 22, owning 42 rental properties, and went bankrupt by age 25. Since then, he has worn the titles of Loan Officer, Realtor, Mega Agent, Team Leader, and International Coach, logging over 600 flights in three years, coaching agents all over North America. His experiences in the varied aspects of real estate and leadership lead him to his movement of helping agents live their best life selling 36 homes a year. He is now the owner and founder of the **National Coaching League.**

Chapter 12

Think Before You Build a Real Estate Team

Let's start with the question, "What made you join Real Estate in the first place?" When I've asked this question, I've found that although the answers may vary, the path is usually predictable.

In the beginning, new agents lack three things: skill set, time on task, and action (aka experimentation). There are many different ways new agents try to compensate for their inexperience in these areas, and one major way is for agents to jump into forming a team.

It's not uncommon for an agent that has early success to realize that there aren't enough hours in the day, so they hire out of pain. But jumping into hiring people in an attempt to share the workload should be the first indicator that the actual need is to slow down.

We've been conditioned to think that more is better, so of course adding team members will only make everyone stronger and make more money, right? What if I argued that the way of the team will not work out for 96% of agents?

Just because someone is a great Real Estate agent doesn't mean that they are a great leader. When an agent decides to form a team, they typically will first hire a buyer's agent to help relieve some of the pressure. Although this often ends up being a great training ground for a new agent, here's where the challenges start to multiply.

Inevitably the already-overwhelmed lead agent is now spending time training instead of producing. The frustration grows as they realize they hired another agent to relieve the stress, and now there is more stress, and, to make it worse, there is NOW less profit.

Let's say they make it through the training of the new buyer's agent and this newly-formed team seems to be chugging right along. Now I'd like to introduce you to "Buyer's Agent Math." They oftentimes forget how much the lead agent has poured into them and start believing their press and start asking for a higher split. Sound familiar? Or, if there is not admin support, what value are they receiving from the lead agent? Did I mention that now the buyer's agent has been the one forming the relationships with your database?

For 96% of agents, their best bet is to build a Business by Relationship™. Let's look at the math: a single agent can typically handle three transactions per month and not move into overwhelm. One of the most common breakdowns of these 36 annual transactions is 24 seller listings, 12 of which also end up being buyers. This has you only working with a total of 24 clients over the course of a year.

In order to do this, as an abundance of deals come in, an agent must raise their standards and be selective about who they work with. This will slow down the pipeline and at the same time produce better results for the clients the agent does say "yes" to. Slow down the pipeline? Yup! See, most agents get into destructive abundance because they don't know their numbers (aka profit and loss), so they subscribe to the philosophy that more is better. But when an agent has eight pending contracts, how proactive do you think they can be on doing the things that got them there in the first place? This is why many agents have a roller coaster of a business.

Think of how nice it would be if you could count on a consistent three closings a month. You can, if you're willing to look at things differently. This is why my program 36 to Life was born. Let's again take a look at the math. If you are building a "Business by Relationship" -- a main component of my 36 to Life program -- inevitably you will see your average sales price increase. My clients who use this system are seeing a sales price increase of between 10% and 25% per year.

Let's say that an agent was able to reach 36 deals per year and their average sales price is $200,000. Based on a 3% commission, that would be $216,000 in GCI. If all things remained the same, meaning the agent continued with closing 36 deals per year, but experienced a 10% increase in sales price each year for the next 5 years, it would look like this:

- Year 1 would bring in an additional $21,600
- Year 2, an additional $51,360
- Year 3, an additional $77,496
- Year 4, an additional $106,245
- Year 5, an additional $137,869

Now here's the cool part: typically the agent's expenses don't go up much with this model. So that's an additional $394,570 in GCI doing the same number of transactions and moving sales price to the $320,000 range. When you look at the stats, I bet there are agents who average a sales price that is 60% above the average new agent price point.

Here's where the real magic happens. As the agent is following and applying this way of building their business, they are also getting more efficient. Their systems are getting dialed in. With only dealing with 24 clients per year (who came by referral because of the "Business by Relationship" model), there's a good chance that the agent will need to be working only part-time.

The next step? Take any additional proceeds and go invest in businesses that are sellable, such as rental properties or other business that have a track record of being easily salable. The reality is that very few Real Estate teams are ever sold for much of anything because there's really not much to sell.

Keep in mind, as Dave Ramsey says, "You can't out-earn stupid." I strongly recommend that you give up debt as you embark on the #36tolife movement. If done properly, most people can find themselves completely debt free in 5-7 years and that's including your mortgage. Unfortunately, most Real Estate agents will end up broke as they never take the time to learn their numbers and have to continue to try and out-earn their bad habits and working 60-70 hours a week or more.

Whether you decide to build a team or run as a solo agent, don't let your ego get in the way -- the plaques and accolades are great, but they don't pay the bills. Remember why you got into Real Estate in the first place.

"Just do it. Imperfect action will beat perfect inaction every single time."

Hank Avink

Scott Hudspeth's

career began as a loan officer in 2003 where he quickly soared to a top closer, closing up to 10 loans a month by his fourth month in the job. Within just two years in this profession, Scott was at the top of his game averaging $25 million annually, helping his clients reach their potential and unlock the opportunities of a lifetime. At one stage, he even closed 42 loans in one month, a huge number within the industry.

Scott's continuous thirst for knowledge and growing expertise led him to want to help others achieve the same heights in the business. Over time he found himself becoming a strategist, coach, mentor, friend, and supporter to thousands of loan officers and real estate agents throughout the US and Canada.

Through his work, Scott has built a company from $170 million in 2013 to over $1 billion in 2016. He now mentors loan officers developing them from Mortgage LO's to Millionaire LO's.

Despite his personal success, Scott remains dedicated to one philosophy. He says: "Helping people to grow and succeed is the only reward needed in life."

If you are looking for more growth, freedom, and coolness in your life and career - don't hesitate to reach out to Scotty and his MLO Team. He is always looking to help people make a change in their lives.

Chapter 13

Marketing To Your Database

I'm Scott Hudspeth with The Marketing Animals and I want to share something with you. We are not in the Real Estate Business, but the business of marketing to our database. I'll share how to best serve your established clients.

Marketing to Your Database

The number one money-making activity you can do is pick up your phone. I recommend that you call everyone in your database three times per year. If you're worried that you haven't talked to someone in a long time, realize that people think about you a whole lot less than you think they do -- just call them!

I recommend that you mark the dates and times for your three calls in your calendar today. The reasons for calling can be: when others are buying/selling homes in their area; during spring and summer; or on special dates to include the time change, closing date anniversary or birthday. If you have more than 300 people in your database, use PhoneBurner.com to place your calls. If you are nervous about calls, I have developed scripts that you can utilize for voicemails or a live calls.

Voicemail Script

"Hey this is <insert name> from <insert company>. I helped you with buying / selling your home in the past. I just wanted to give you a quick thanks for letting me help out. If you ever have any real estate or mortgage questions, or would like a report on home prices in your neighborhood, please give me a buzz. By the way, I was just looking at some home values in your area and I think you will be pleased with what I have to show you. The best number to reach me at is <insert phone number>. Hope all is well, and hope to talk to you soon. Oh, also, if you have any friends or family members that could use some honest help, just give me a call about that too, I would be honored to help out. I'll talk to you when you call back. Bye."

Live Answer Script

"Hey this is <insert name> from <insert company>. I helped you with buying / selling your home in the past. I just wanted to give you a quick thanks for letting me help out. How are you guys doing? <pause for answer and give an appropriate response> If you ever have any real estate or mortgage questions, please give me a buzz. If you will grab a pen, I'll give you my number. <give time for them to get a pen> The best number to reach me at is <insert phone number>. Hope all is well, and hope to talk to you soon. Oh, also, do you have any friends or family members that are looking to buy, sell, or refinance a home and could use some honest help? <pause for answer>. Can I count on you to give me a call when you do? I would be honored to help out. I'll talk to you when you call back. Bye."

These phone calls should be about 2-3 minutes long and are all about the client. If they ask about you, just say "Great thanks," and shift the focus back to them. Imagine what your business would look like if you made an additional 300 calls a month, and it all took a total of about 5 hours or about 1 hour and 15 minutes a week!

Reaching Out Via Email

Studies have shown that emailing once a week provides the highest response rate, click rate and less opt-outs versus emailing once a month.

Here is the key though -- don't send real estate information all the time because it's boring. You can occasionally send out market info, but don't ever send out one listing to your entire database. Instead go for fun, social emails and sprinkle in real estate.

A key to successful emails is video marketing, which I call the social lubricant. When your audience sees you once a week, it's like you gave them a shot of tequila before talking real estate. Additionally, think of a favorite movie star. Whether or not you have met him/her, you feel like you know them, because of the power of video. Create that same celebrity effect for yourself. All it takes is a video, shot with your smartphone in one take, about 60-90 seconds in length with a short call to action.

The email topic I found that works the best is to incorporate it with a video of "What's happening in your community this weekend." I search local events on Google, pick three short easy things, and produce a video. For example, "Hi, this is ___ from ABC Realty. Here are some of the cool things we've found to do this weekend (list events), we hope to see you there! Remember, if you're looking to buy, sell or refinance a home, that's what we do. Give us a call! See ya out on the town!" Make emails short, sweet, easy-to-read and double space.

My tips for video:
- Keep it simple, one shot will suffice
- No editing
- No bumper music
- Shoot outside around a "nature scene" or in front of one of your listings
- Post it on YouTube

If you decide to edit your email, outsource it to a professional from Fiverr. They can create what I call a "video sandwich." It includes an introduction, a 30-40 second viral video, and then your call to action. For example: "Hey this is Scott, at ABC realty, check this out. (Insert 30-40 second viral video) Wasn't that funny? I just love those kinds of things. If you're looking to buy or sell, contact me."

Videos are especially effective when you team up with a loan officer or insurance agent, and send to their database as well. Remember, just be yourself, and have fun with it!

Best Days/Times to Send

Know that some people will opt out, and that is okay. Focus on your fans. If you get a 14% open rate, that is successful. Don't leave all the wealth on the table based on the fear that everybody is opting out.

According to a MailChimp survey:
- Weekly emails are the best to send, with the lowest opt-out rate
- The highest open and click rates happen on Saturday
- The number one day to unsubscribe is Tuesday
- Emails sent first thing in the morning have the highest click through rate

Snail Mail

I recommend that you send out a monthly mailer, but it's not going to be what you think. You send out four types of mailers, once per month, and then repeat the cycle three times.

- **Month one** - From the mind of the greatest salesperson, Joe Girard, send out a simple "I like you." I hand write it in blue ink, have it photocopied and utilize a hand-written envelope. It's a very effective mailing and I recommend hiring high school kids at 10-20 cents per piece to address the envelope. If you have 300 people, it costs $30-60. This is a very effective mailing.
- **Month two** - The second mailing is what I call the "Superman letter." You share a success where a client had a problem and you ripped off your shirt and helped them. The letter is about the recipient, yet in everybody's subconscious mind, they'll realize that you can help them. It's social proof. Do it in Word, use a live signature in blue ink, make color copies and send it out.
- **Month three** -- I like you (same as month one).
- **Month four** - This fourth mailing is proof that "I'm a real person, just like you." It's like the holiday recap letter where you tell a happy, nostalgic story that shows your human side. Type up this feel-good letter, use a blue signature, color copy and mail it out.

When you're ready to build your business -- take action! Make calls, send video emails and follow up with this creative snail mail system. If you do any one of these three things, you'll get more business, and if you combine all three, you'll enjoy monstrous results.

"Think of a favorite movie star. Whether or not you have met him/her, you feel like you know them, because of the power of video."

Scott Hudspeth

*Meet the Olivia Pope
of branding.*

Kelly Lucente is

a CEO, Author and Brand Strategist who focuses on growing small to Fortune 500 brands, assisting them in differentiating themselves to move the needle through strategic brand positioning. She is the Founder and Creative Director of Re-Tool Marketing (RTM), a boutique corporate branding agency in Minneapolis, MN and CEO of Brand By Kelly, the small business and entrepreneurial branding branch of RTM. She recently launched her own networking organization, Think-osophy, which puts a twist on the old-fashioned ways of networking.

With 30 years' experience in marketing and sales, Kelly is known for her disruptive approach to getting brands noticed. She has worked with nationally noteworthy brands such as **RE/ MAX, Pearle Vision, Rollerblade,** and **Mattamy Homes,** North America's largest home builder.

Kelly is the author of MOO-LAH-GY, a handbook for the entrepreneur and small business owner which offers practical solutions to frequently asked questions within the brand and positioning space.

Chapter 14

How to Create a Personal Brand

Here is a big secret -- you already are a brand. Everyone has a personal brand whether you do anything about it or not. I frequently state that doing a little work on yours and seeing how everyone responds can be an eye-opener.

I am brand strategist and I am here to help you win. Win against your competition who claim they do exactly what you do, and tell everyone that they can do it better. I can help you set the record straight and remove them from the equation.

I will show you how to build a personal brand that will define and solidify your reputation in your industry and help you close or convert on business and sales that you seek!

Here is how:
- Why personal brand is such a big deal
- The difference between a personal and a corporate brand
- Brand stats that you need to know
- The Power of 3: Image + Voice + Promise = Personal Brand

- How LinkedIn can be one of your most useful branding tools

People think branding is about graphic design and logos, but it's not. Branding is about one thing: *perception*. It's an instinctual vibe that people feel about you, what you sell, or your style. And it's something, believe it or not, that you can control.

I've been asked often if my brand is personal or corporate. My answer is always "It depends on one thing: Do you want the brand to survive you?" If you're hit by a bus, do you want your business to be a legacy that can be transferred to someone else: a business partner, a child, or a spouse? Do you plan to have a team? Will there be more people on your payroll or will the buck stop with you? These questions have to be answered for me to advise someone on which way to go.

When real estate agents want to work with a broker, I want them to think about the stigmas attached to that broker. There are perceptions made about every brand that—when you work with them—that can become stuck to yours. I would highly recommend that every real estate agent have a personal brand because it's probably unlikely that you will retire after working with a single brokerage. So, what you don't want to do is have too much of an identity attachment to the brokerage brand because you want your sphere of influence to continue to follow *you.*

Corporate versus Personal Branding

I want you to remember something: the size of your audience doesn't matter. What's important is that the audience is listening. It's very important when you're branding that you have people that *get* the brand. Corporate branding is very much a 'They' game. You market *to* your audience and constantly adjust the brand assets and your marketing techniques to meet your audience's expectations so that they feel heard. *They* dictate a lot of how corporate brands move and evolve.

Personal brand, on the other hand, is a 'We' game. It's how *we* feel about things: our favorite color, or our point of view. Once you get a strong handle on how you show up and why you're the optimal choice, then you attract the people who want more of that.

It's all about the message that you push out to prove that you're relevant. It takes two things to stay relevant. Number one: proof of concept. Do you do what you claim you do? And number two: social proof. And that's everyone who's talking about it, raving about you, and the referrals that come from it.

Fast Company put out a statistic that says there's a clear correlation between success and branding. *Entrepreneur Magazine* likewise said that you get 561% more reach if an employee shares the company brand message, as it's shared 24 times more frequently. Also, employees have ten times more followers, and they receive eight times more engagement on a post. What does this mean? It's about their personal brand, not the company brand. It's about the individual pushing out the information about what they sell and getting more engagement than the corporate brand page. Companies that *don't* get their employees involved on social media are absolutely losing out to companies that do.

The Brand of You
Can you describe yourself? Let's say I have a problem that needs to be solved. Tell me why I would pick you?

Jeff Bezos, Amazon's CEO, has this to say about your personal brand, "Your brand is what other people say about you when you're not in the room." When people hear your name, what do they think about you? That's your brand, in a nutshell.

The key here is differentiation. In a commoditized space, you don't necessarily need to be able to tell people that *nobody* can do what you do. Sometimes, already established relationships will be in place so you are going to need more to separate you from a sea of the same.

A few questions I want you to think about:
- What is your personal vision?
- What do you see for your life?
- What is your personal purpose?
- Why were you put on this earth?
- What's your personal mission?
- How do *you* plan to make a difference?

The point to personal branding is that you need to know yourself well. Know your strengths. Take people that you admire and respect and ask them what they think you're known for. If their answers are a disconnect from what you want to be known for, then you have some work to do.

The Power of Three

There are three essential ingredients to your personal brand that I want to share with you to help you think about how to boost yours.

Image

How do you show up? This is important because people can be unaware of how others perceive them. You need to have a professional headshot, that is not negotiable. You need to consider how you show up online: your digital footprint. If you have a LinkedIn account, it's going to be one of the top results when people Google you. Make sure it comes across as professional and leaves the impression you desire.

Voice

This takes into consideration both verbal and non-verbal communication skills. It's how you appear through your summary and description on LinkedIn, your emails, personal greetings, and your overall tone, execution, dialogue and vernacular. All of that is attached to your brand.

Promise

Why YOU over any other real estate agent? Think about what happens *because* of you. How do you add value? If I work with you, what should I expect to happen?

And that's it! Keep your online profiles updated and professional and make sure to highlight the best of your personal brand! Make sure you go back and do a brand audit, answering all of the questions I've asked. Incorporate your answers and you *will* have a surefire way to take control of your brand.

"When people hear your name, what do they think about you? That's your brand, in a nutshell."

Kelly Lucente

Richard Smith

helps Loan Officers and Real Estate Agents grow their business to 10x levels and, have more freedom. He is a national speaker, coach, author and co-founder of Remote Assistant Scout, a firm that helps Real Estate Agents hire virtual assistants to grow their business and have more freedom. Richard also is a Branch Manager for Success Mortgage Partners and lives in Katy, Texas.

Chapter 15

Finding, Hiring and Utilizing Virtual Assistants!

Do you find yourself engaging in non-money-making activities and you'd like to find quality employees to assist you? I'm Richard Smith, a loan officer, and I have successfully mastered the art of finding, hiring and utilizing Virtual Assistants (VA). My team is comprised of remote employees who work around the world. I've built a successful business by offloading non-money-making activities to my team.

Why Hire a Virtual Assistant?

A VA is an office administration professional offering remote administrative, technical, or creative support to any small to medium business, and are a must for massive growth. Hiring a VA reduces operating costs, increases productivity and provides freedom. The average VA salary costs $4/hour versus $15/hour for an in-house employee. With a VA there is no need to:

- Increase your office space
- Hire a full-time employee

- Worry about sick leaves
- Pay for vacation
- Worry about employee benefits
- Worry about high salaries

Steps to Hiring a Virtual Assistant

1. **Define your job description.** Write down each task and the amount of time required to perform them. Detail the workload in writing to select the right person for your business. Include a brief description of your business in the job post to help job seekers better align their experiences with your business and job opening.

2. **Post your VA ad or work with online firms.** Organizations like Upwork, OnlineJobs.ph, E-Lance, Freelancers.com and Guru have done most of the guesswork for you.

3. **Prepare for the interview.** Require a DISC Personality profile assessment. Write out your interview questions ahead of time and establish what you want to know about your prospective employee. Practice asking the questions and consider what types of responses you need.

4. **The interview.** The virtual nature of the position means that applicants could come from anywhere in the world, and you can use tools such as Skype, Viber Video and Google Hangouts to interview applicants. Select 3-5 applicants who have met ALL of your criteria for interview and go to a quiet place where you can give your undivided attention. If working on your time zone is important to you, set the meeting on your time zone. Be on the lookout for red flags -- applicants who are eager to be hired will go to

the interview on time and without excuses. If the interviews go well, select your top two candidates. Give the top two candidates a second interview.

5. **Welcome your new VA.** Make him/her feel a part of the team by writing a welcome message, or having a call with them on their first day. Set expectations, not hard lines, and don't fail to do this very important step! The more time you invest on the front end, the more effective your VA will be when it is in operations mode. Clarify the role and job description of your new virtual assistant.

6. **Train your virtual assistant.** Dedicate the first week for your virtual assistant to familiarize with his/her roles. Have them utilize training tools as part of their job.

Example Ad Template

"Looking for a full time Virtual Assistant that must be able to think quickly and handle multiple tasks at once. You will be responsible for managing the ins and outs of a web-based Client Relationship Management System, all Social Media and online marketing tools including Facebook, Linkedin, Twitter and YouTube, video marketing and editing of videos, uploading of property information to a single property website system and some phone support.

MUST be able to work between 9am and 5pm Central Standard Time. Must be able to give 40 hours FULL TIME and have NO other job. Dedicated computer with wired Internet Access is required. Knowing Microsoft Word and Google Docs is a BIG plus, but not required as long as you are willing and eager to learn. MUST speak excellent English.

To apply for this position, please reply to this post with your resume, contact information (including Skype ID), a sample voice recording, and a preferred time for an interview."

Beginner's Tools After Hiring a VA

Once your VA is hired, I recommend these key tools to operate smoothly:

- **Asana.** Create an account in Asana (www.app.asana.com) and invite your virtual assistant via his/her email address. Asana is the best team management tool that you can use in assigning tasks, their deadlines and tracking progress. Require your virtual assistant to provide daily recaps in Asana.
- **Skype.** Create a new Skype account dedicated to your virtual assistant for work hours as your main medium of communication. Skype offers unlimited calling subscriptions and a local mobile number that your virtual assistant can utilize for calling leads, clients, realtors and business partners. PhoneBurner is a power dialer that dials prospects, instantly leaves voicemail messages, and sends follow-up emails automatically, and I recommend it for large databases.
- **Jing.** (www.techsmith.com/jing) is a great tool for creating training videos that captures and records anything you see on your computer screen and lets you share it instantly.
- **Animoto.** (www.animoto.com) is a platform for creating and customizing videos from photos and video clips. This is a great tool your VA can use in creating virtual tours for your realtor partners. You can also share videos from Animoto instantly!
- **Hootsuite.** Hootsuite connects up to 50 social accounts and offers a birds-eye view of all of them.

Your VA can schedule posts and reply in real time, which increases productivity.

- **BombBomb.** Build relationships and stay in touch with your clients and realtor contacts through video email marketing with BombBomb (www.bombbomb.com). With this tool, your VA can easily create, send rich video emails, simple video messages, or even traditional text and image emails and track all the results of both traditional and video emails. BombBomb lets you send individual emails or an entire series of emails automatically.

What do you have your new VA do?
1. **Social Media Marketing**
   Social Media Set Up and Optimization
   Social Media Content Postings
   Run and Manage Facebook Ads
   Birthday Greetings
2. **Blogging**
   Moderate and Content Posting to Wordpress and to ActiveRain Blog
3. **Outbound Phone Calls**
   Expired Listings
   Past Clients
   Circle Prospecting
   Client Follow Up
   Transaction Coordination
4. **E-mail Marketing and Correspondence**
   Automated Email Marketing
   Past Clients
   Set Right Email Campaigns
5. **Search Engine Optimization**
   Set Up Online Business Listings
   Business Review Solicitation

Back Linking
Google Authorship, AdWords and Analytics

6. **Website Management**
Basic Website Designing
Content Moderation
Contact Information Updates
Renewal of Domains and Web Hosting

7. **Miscellaneous Tasks**
Open House Flyer Creation
Content Blogging
Database and Contact Updates
Postcard and Brochures Creation
Landing Page and Website Domain Set Up

Other Details To Note

To pay your VA, you can use Paypal, Western Union, Transfast, RemitLy and Zoom. Never, ever should you be late when paying your virtual assistant.

If and when it comes time to terminate a VA, keep this in mind. Sometimes, no matter how well you prepare and follow the Virtual Assistant Lifecycle, things just don't work out. Don't feel guilty. You terminate a VA the moment you think about doing so.

No matter where you are in your business, a VA has the power to declutter your workload and free you up to concentrate on doing what you do best – sell! After all, if you're not out selling, no one is doing it on your behalf.

Hire a Virtual Assistant: ALL DONE FOR YOU

Finding and hiring the right worker for your business takes a lot of valuable time and effort, so instead of being overwhelmed with recruiting, we want you to focus on the more important aspects of your business like making sales and leave all the work to *Remote Assistant Scout*. Just tell them what type of worker you're looking for and they'll take it from there and handle every step of recruiting your next virtual worker.

Remote Assistant Scout is boutique firm co-founded by Richard Smith that helps mortgage loan officers and real estate agents have the best fit virtual assistant through a comprehensive scouting and screening process. If you're in the market of hiring your own virtual assistant and would like more information regarding the ALL DONE FOR YOU services of Remote Assistant Scout, call (281) 394-0624 or e-mail rsmith@realestateagentsupport.com.

"A VA has the power to declutter your workload and free you up to concentrate on doing what you do best – sell!"

Richard Smith

Amy Broghamer

is a Realtor in Cincinnati, Ohio and Northern Kentucky. Her small team, The Amy B Sells Team, is made up of herself, a Master Listing Specialist, and Expert Buyer Agent, Jenny. Amy and Jenny have both been in the business for more than 12 years each, and are ranked in the top 1% of Cincinnati Realtors. The team sells around 50 homes a year and around 12M in sales, and focuses on Referral only business.

Amy is the creator of the online course "Sell 100% of your Listings" and "The Ultimate Buyer Loyalty Process," which catapulted her into the limelight as an instructor and trainer and national speaker for Real Estate. As of late, she is seen as an expert on using Video in your Business, and is often found on Live Facebook feeds and YouTube videos sharing how Realtors can use video to set themselves apart, and convert leads faster.

Amy has proudly created a schedule where she can work Monday - Friday from 7:30-4:30, so she can spend time with her husband and two little boys.

Chapter 16

The Ultimate Buyer Loyalty Process

How would you like to double your income, reduce your stress and work with buyers that you truly like?

I'm Amy Broghamer and I have trained many Buyers Agents with the tools I'll share with you. Each time, the agent walks away at least doubling his or her annual income. Not only does their income increase, but their stress levels and frustration with clients is reduced significantly.

I learned these skills through my expertise from a 13-year career as a Realtor, where I earned more than $100M in career sales. I'm a CRS, ABR, RPAC Major Investor, and Author of the online courses "The Ultimate Buyer Loyalty Process" and "Sell 100% of your Listings." I operate a small team powered by EXP Realty in Cincinnati, OH, with myself as a Master Listing Specialist, and an Expert Buyer Specialist.

I'd like to share a story with you.

When Jenny came to my team she had been in the real estate industry for over 10 years. Jenny was only averaging an annual income of $40k per year, after a full decade in the industry. As they say, she was having her first year, every year. Recognizing Jenny's potential, I made her my Expert Buyer's Specialist who focused only on buyers, and required that she follow my standards and the system I created called "The Ultimate Buyer Loyalty Process."

Jenny followed everything that I'm going to share with you, and you'll love her results. The first year with me, she doubled her income by earning $80k in commission. In her second year, she earned $120k, completely tripling her initial income that she had grown accustomed to in the previous ten years. What Jenny needed was to have systems and tools in place. Once she did, she raved that she earned a lot more money, experienced a lot less stress and now works with buyers she likes.

I'll share with you how to:
1. Set standards for working with buyers.
2. Obtain the 3 key components to elevate buyers to VIP status.
3. Identify how to work with buyers you LIKE and reduce your stress as a result.

Demonstrating Value as an Agent

I want to share that as a professional, the more value you add, the more valuable you'll become. Let's look at the definition of value -- it's the regard that something is held to deserve; the importance, worth or usefulness of something. So you may be wondering, "How do I demonstrate my value to clients?"

First and foremost, position yourself as the expert and demonstrate to buyers that you are the leader and the professional. Share your standards and expectations and have convictions for your standards. Communicate your experience as an agent and highlight your core values that buyers desire.

What are these core values sought out by buyers? According to the NAR 2017 Profile of Home Buyers and Sellers, those that topped the list included honesty, integrity, responsiveness, knowledge of the purchase process and knowledge of the real estate market.

As you can see, high standards are the key to being desirable as an agent. Have you thought about setting standards for your clients as well?

Setting Standards for Clients

I want to share a simple truth: standards solve problems. What standards have you set for yourself in your business related to buyers? Many agents may find this to be an unusual question. We often, especially when we're first starting out, will work with anyone and everyone, which can lead to lots of time and effort spent on our part, without conversion. We work with clients who don't have the money, aren't clear on what they're looking for, and we end up exhausted and stressed as a result.

In The Ultimate Buyer Loyalty Process, and in my business, we have set three non-negotiable keys to buyer loyalty. If a client is unable to check off all three things on this list, we don't work with them.

We communicate directly with clients and let them know, in a clear, approachable and personable way, that there are three steps they'll need to take before we help them find their dream home. We communicate these standards via email with pre-recorded videos, on the phone, and in person at our counseling session.

Three Keys To Buyer Loyalty

Add these to your business model and you will find that they simplify and streamline your operations -- they solve problems. Clients must have these three items checked off the list in order to work with us:

- **Be pre-approved with a trusted lender**. I don't work with people who aren't pre-approved. We take it one step further and recommend our trusted lender. If a potential client tells you that they aren't going to get pre-approved for a loan before working with you, then move on. That's a big red flag.
- **Have a buyer consultation.** After our client receives pre-approval, we sit down for a buyer consultation. Before we set it up, we email a video explaining what to expect and that they will sign two forms during the consultation. To expedite the process, we link to both forms in the video. During the consultation we handle introductions, ask questions to learn what our clients are looking for, discuss finance options, the buying process, get contact information, schedule a tour and have them sign our buyer loyalty agreement.
- **Hire expert buyer's specialist.** Some states require buyers agency agreements, so take it upon yourself to figure out how to sign a contract with a buyer as step three. When meeting with the client, discuss expectations, and educate them about commission. Once we have a client complete this third step, 9/10 have a pen in hand and sign on with us.

Our Conversion Rate
97% of the time when our buyer lead follows these three steps, we close on a property for them. Why not 100%?

Some people in the middle of the process, get married and have new needs, relocate with a new job, etc. But wouldn't you say that 97% is incredibly impressive?

When compared to those who don't set standards for buyers, it's safe to say that most buyers are only 50% committed, and agents are running around with people who aren't even qualified for a home loan. Wouldn't you rather demonstrate your value and have clients more than willing to work with you on your terms?

When you give great service, have standards and are professional, you will deliver a great home buying experience. Additionally, you'll create a thrilled, loyal buyer who will refer you many times and you'll never need online leads again. Those are the best and most profitable kinds of buyers you can have -- referrals.

If you stay in your comfort zone, you're never going to grow. I encourage you to follow these three standards, and dig deeper into my Ultimate Buyer Loyalty Process System to set standards, earn more money, enjoy a rewarding experience and work with buyers you like.

"The more value you add, the more valuable you become."

Amy Broghamer

When **Char Klisares** jumped into the real estate industry, she created a ripple of change. She wrote 32 transactions her first year, 52 her second, and 71 her third year, and rapidly became a trusted expert in the industry. The necessity for leverage was felt immediately. So when  the traditional team model didn't work, she created The One Agent Team. Based in servant leadership and coming from contribution she found an effective way to "GO BIG, by going small."

The One Agent Team completely revamps how real estate leveraging is done. It provides a better experience by creating win/win relationships for the buyer, seller, buyer's agent, listing agent, loan office and real estate broker. This model takes little down time to implement with no overhead cost. It proves you can make money, grow your business and create a better industry at the same time.

Char proudly practices real estate through RE/Max Hilltop in Des Moines, Iowa. She's won multiple production awards including the Circle of Excellence. She's mother to three amazing young adults, Makenzie, Jonathan and Ryleigh. Char regularly coaches, mentors and assist new agents, entrepreneurs and local business leaders. Char is an inspirational speaker, domestic violence advocate and founder of the CKRET Foundation, whose focus is bringing awareness, funding and change to domestic violence.

Chapter 17

One Agent Team

Buyers don't just wake up and purchase a house because they're bored. There's typically a life event that happens. Good or bad - it creates a need. **This** is where a real estate transaction really starts. Being aware of what they are going through, I made sure to focus on minimizing surprises, providing timely responses and checking in with how they are doing. I treat my clients the way I would want to be treated, and they become like family.

Now don't get me wrong - I hold the dollar accountable. I take business very seriously. I spend a lot of time and money training, reading, learning and growing mindset. I hire coaches to push, challenge and hold me accountable. I track numbers, implement systems and follow known metrics that work. I'm always open to change, feedback and outside-the-box ideas.

When I first jumped into real estate, it was just me and a very reliable closing coordinator. When I hit 30 transactions, I hired a full-time admin. They were responsible for ALL paperwork, emails, scheduling, phone calls and logistics. This allowed more time for me to help people and grow the business. We quickly added a field runner and a virtual assistant allowing my admin to leverage routine task and responsibilities.

At first, I helped anyone and everyone. I worked a lot. I had my PhD in real estate, yet in reality -- I was poor, hungry and desperate. As we mastered leveraging, the demand for

MY time created the next obstacle. With only 24 hours in a day, there were some things I couldn't leverage, like sleeping, eating, and family time. With the help of a business coach we looked for what would give the most bang for the time. It didn't take long to find the leverage position in real estate is with LISTINGS. Listings have a 5:1 return ratio. I could help five sellers in the same amount of time it took to help one buyer. With predictable results, I got very purposeful with my time. If I had to choose between helping a seller or buyer -- I took the listing.

When I didn't follow up with a buyer lead, they immediately moved on to another agent - this is typical and NOT personal. These people are going through something and need help NOW. I wanted to make sure the buyer got connected with an agent who was available to take care of them now. Because I was too busy to do anything with these leads, I asked a few preferred lenders if they'd be willing to help. I'd pass buyer leads onto them knowing with the promise of quickly connecting them with an agent who could help. NO strings or referral fees attached. *Imagine a real estate agent who's NOT asking a lender for leads but giving leads to a lender?* I didn't realize how outside-the-box thinking this was at the time - I was simply taking care of people.

With the continued growth of my business, I decided to implement a traditional team model by adding buyer's agents. I offered unlimited access to resources, staff, coaching and myself. My intent was good in theory, yet executing this plan turned into a horrible mess. I found myself working longer days, babysitting agents and helping fewer clients while completely pulled out of production. My business incurred unnecessary risks and expenses, metrics were unsustainable, clients were complaining, and I was miserable. After six months I pulled the plug and dissolved the team. The agents were angry and disappointed, yet I was relieved.

When the dust settled, it hit me -- **LEVERAGE, LEVERAGE, LEVERAGE!** I could leverage everyone involved in a transaction -- to do what they are currently doing in a way that would benefit ALL of us.

Implementing The One Agent Team:

As a top producing real estate agent, I have an endless stream of lenders asking for referral business. The lenders are the most important part of real estate transactions, because without the money, we don't have a sale. The lenders also know who the good agents are. They see firsthand who does a good job of servicing their clients vs. collecting a paycheck. Knowing this, I thought, *"I want to leverage THAT!"*

STEP 1:
Meet new lenders weekly - Time block the same day and time
Ask your lenders for names of really good agents, of whom they are currently working with, and who could use more business. Agents can be from any brokerage.

STEP 2:
Meet new agents weekly - Time block the same day and time
This is a mini group interview, so keep it light. YOU are sharing an amazing opportunity. Make sure you feel comfortable and the agent is capable of representing you! If everything aligns, share the app used to field leads, information about a weekly group coaching call, and clarify expectations about the accountability spreadsheets. End by teaching the script to use when following up with a new lead.

STEP 3:

Set up Buyer Board - This is your TEAM!

GroupMe is a FREE mobile app. It is super easy to add and remove people, create multiple environments, integrate with your mobile calendar, and it allows pdf and photo sharing, and more.

STEP 4:

Hold weekly group coaching call - This is where the magic happens!

I use FreeConferenceCall.com. Using a toll-free number, everyone dials in at the scheduled time. Calls are usually an hour long. I focus on educating how to get better conversion rates, handle objections or known real estate strategies. I ask them to share success stories and often have a local home inspector, lender, broker or real estate professional join us. Every month, I make one of the calls mandatory. It keeps my board fresh.

LEAD MANAGEMENT

As leads come in, my admin or virtual assistant sends a message in the GroupMe environment asking who's available. The agent who responds first will get a private message with lead information or instructions. We expect immediate follow up. I also field the buyer leads I receive throughout my day via the app. We field leads 24/7.

ACCOUNTABILITY SPREADSHEET
THIS IS IMPORTANT

If you don't track it, you can't be held accountable for it. So once a week, my virtual assistant updates the agents' personal spreadsheets with the leads that were accepted. These spreadsheets are to be updated with the current status every Monday. I review for topics to discuss on our weekly coaching call.

REFERRAL FEE STRUCTURE:

I create two different environments. With the sheer volume of leads, I do not fill out a referral form until I know they're a sale. Labeling the rooms help remove any doubt of what I expect.

- **25% Referral Fee to Char Klisares**
  I have not spent any time with these leads. They can be sign calls, internet leads, Google voice, marketing calls, etc.
- **50% Referral Fee to Char Klisares**
  I have spent time with these leads. They are usually pre-approved and I've done a preliminary buyer interview. They are typically a referral or someone I am currently working with.

Once the environment is created you can easily add or remove people. I periodically perform audits of agents' productions to keep everyone honest. We've learned that by leveraging the lenders in search of great agents, this hasn't been a problem.

BENEFITS TO BROKER:

Their agents receive FREE leads, coaching and training. Their agents network with other top agents, and they get a split of the business from the agent.

BENEFITS TO LOAN OFFICER:

It's FREE, grows production numbers and relationships with other agents. It builds valuable relationships with listing agents, and saves thousands of marketing dollars, instead of paying companies like Zillow.

Loan officers should implement this model for their own business!

BENEFITS TO BUYER:
No conflict of interest, quick follow up, and working with a knowledgeable agent who's mentored by a top producer. It partners them with an advocate who will slow down and provide education of the process.

BENEFITS TO BUYER AGENT:
It's FREE - NO risk. There is free coaching and training, Open House opportunities, and the ability to work and network with other good agents. Agents are allowed to use the board if they need help. Agents can be on multiple agent's boards at the same time with no conflict of interest. Quality of life improves, and if you are busy, it's ok, there will be another opportunity.

BENEFITS TO LISTING AGENT:
NO babysitting, overhead, and it's easy to add and remove agents. Only branding team name and self. No Risk - if the market shifts, I can shut the board down. It only takes three to five hours a week to run, with no training. You can handpick agents to receive hot leads, quality of life improves, and the Law of Reciprocity with lenders and buyer's agents occurs, which benefits clients.

BENEFITS TO A SELLER:
No conflict of interest, ALL leads are followed up on immediately, and I ONLY focused on getting them SOLD.

The only buyers I work with are MY SELLERS who are looking. Outside of our scheduled tours, I make the promise of getting them inside ANY listing they want to see within two hours (sellers permitting). I then handpick the BEST agent from my team. I pay a 25% referral if my client closes on a listing they showed OR $20 an hour for their time -- either way, they are getting paid! I make it very clear, they are strictly a showing agent, and I will do everything else.

THE ONE AGENT TEAM - BUILDER MODULE
How would you like to get paid on what you build AND what your competitor builds? With The One Agent Team Builder module it's possible.

THE ONE AGENT TEAM - INVESTOR MODULE
Real estate agents and investors have a long history of a love/hate relationship. Would you like to even the playing field with an agent who has equal skin in YOUR game? With The One Agent Team Investor Module it's possible.

DO YOU HAVE QUESTIONS OR WANT MORE INFORMATION?
The One Agent Team can be found on Facebook or YouTube. Char Klisares believes in being the change you wish to see in the world, and by sharing The One Agent Team model for FREE, it will create a better industry, one closing at a time!

"Once I stopped chasing the dollar, the dollars found me!"

Char Klisares

Join Agent Mastermind Today!

www.facebook.com/groups/AgentMastermind

Made in the USA
Lexington, KY
18 November 2018